Storybook Classrooms

Using Children's Literature In the Learning Center

Humanics Limited * Atlanta, Georgia

For Tom,

Who knows all the reasons why.

HUMANICS LIMITED
P. O. Box 7447
Atlanta, Georgia 30309

Library of Congress
Card Catalog Number: 83 -81430

PRINTED IN THE
UNITED STATES OF AMERICA

ISBN: 0 - 89334 - 043 - X

Fourth Printing 1987

"Jump or Jiggle" from *Another Here and Now Story Book* by Lucy Sprague Mitchell. Copyright © 1937 by E. P. Dutton. Copyright renewal © 1965 by Lucy Sprague Mitchell. Reprinted by permission of the publisher, E. P Dutton.

"Easy Honey Candy" and "Honey Gingerbread Cookies" from *The Pooh Cook Book* by Virginia H. Ellison. Copyright © 1969 by Daphne Dorothy Milne and Spencer Curtis Brown. Reprinted by permission of the publisher, E. P. Dutton, Inc.

"Barefoot" from *Still More Small Poems* by Valerie Worth, pictures by Natalie Babbitt. Poems copyright © 1976, 1977, 1978 by Valerie Worth. Pictures copyright © 1978 by Natalie Babbitt. Reprinted by permission of Farrar, Straus and Giroux, Inc.

"The Little Turtle" from *Johnny Appleseed and Other Poems* by Vachel Lindsay. Copyright © 1920 by Macmillan Publishing Co., Inc., renewed 1948 by Elizabeth C. Lindsay. Reprinted with permission of Macmillan.

"I Met A Man Who Was Playing Games" from *I Met A Man* by John Ciardi. Copyright © 1961 by John Ciardi. Reprinted by permission of Houghton Mifflin Company.

Nonsense Alphabet" from *The Complete Nonsense Book* by Edward Lear. Copyright © 1946 by Dodd, Mead & Co. Reprinted by permission of Dodd, Mead & Co.

Table of Contents

INTRODUCTION — 1

CHAPTER ONE — 3
Why Literature Learning Centers?

CHAPTER TWO — 9
How to Construct, Manage and Evaluate Learning Centers

CHAPTER THREE — 23
Folklore
Folk and Fairy Tales
Fables
Pourquoi Stories

CHAPTER FOUR — 51
Fantasy
Fantasy Involving Human Characters
Animal Fantasy

CHAPTER FIVE — 95
Exceptional Children

CHAPTER SIX — 103
Poetry

CHAPTER SEVEN — 125
Concept and Informational Books

CHAPTER EIGHT — 161
Reading Readiness
Counting Books
Alphabet Books
Mother Goose

CHAPTER NINE   **191**
Wordless Books

CHAPTER TEN   **213**
The Art of Picture Books
Illustrators and Their Work

INTRODUCTION

Storybook Classrooms· Using Children's Literature in the Learning Center is intended for teachers of kindergarten through third grade; however, some of the suggested activities may be adapted to other levels. The majority of the activities recommended in this book are to be done independently by the children, in keeping with the learning center format. Because of the importance of small and large group interaction in the primary grades, ideas for teacher directed activities have also been included.

The focus of this book is on the use of children's literature in the classroom. The success of such a program is dependent upon the provision of a wide variety of books for the children to read and upon the reading of books *to* the children on a regular basis. Suggestions for creative expression in art, writing, and drama are included here. Since skills are an integral part of the reading program in the primary grades, activities for word identification and comprehension have also been included. The skills activities, however, *do* reflect the themes of specific books.

The content of *Storybook Classrooms· Using Children's Literature in the Learning Center* is organized around the following areas: Chapter 1 provides a rationale for using literature in the classroom and for learning centers as a means of classroom management. Chapter 2 discusses ways of organizing centers and offers suggestions for preparing games and activities. Chapters 3 and 4 focus on folklore and fantasy as types of literature and recommend numerous activities for independent work with books in these areas. Chapter 5 is somewhat different from the other sections in the book in that it deals with an understanding and awareness of exceptional children through *group* interaction by using literature. Very general suggestions that can be adapted to fit the unique situations in different classrooms are given in this chapter. Chapter 6 also departs from the traditional learning center concept because of the nature of the topic: poetry. In the primary grades, poetry can be dealt with best through much reading aloud to the children and through activities to foster appreciation. Some independent work with poetry is suggested here, but most activities are intended for group participation. Chapters 7, 8, and 9 deal with concept and informational books; books for "readiness," including counting, alphabet, and Mother Goose; and wordless books. Many activities for independent work are recommended in these sections. The purpose of Chapter 10 is to suggest ways in which both teachers and students can gain insight into the art of picture books and the people who create them. Both professional resources and recommendations for student activities are included.

It is hoped that the many activities for child involvement suggested in *Storybook Classrooms: Using Children's Literature in the Learning Center* and the extensive bibliographies in each chapter will assist in the development of wide recreational reading by all students.

K.H.W.
M.J.G.

CHAPTER ONE

Why
Literature Learning
Centers?

Values of Literature

Children of all ages enjoy being read to. Educators generally agree on the desirability of reading aloud to children and encouraging them to read independently. Too often, however, time during the school day is not allotted for activities to foster recreational reading. The only contact many children have with reading is their classroom instruction. For some, this experience is a difficult and personally unrewarding one. To these children, reading consists of drill on skills, answering detailed questions, and orally struggling through a passage. Such an experience is not likely to perpetuate reading as a lifelong habit. Literature possesses qualities and values that cannot be supplied by any other area of the curriculum. As Huck (1979) said, "Most of what a child studies at school is concerned with learning skills or facts, only literature is concerned with thoughts and feelings" (p. 700).

Listening to entertaining and well-written stories is a pleasurable experience for children. It is an experience which children should learn to associate with the act of reading long before formal reading instruction is begun. In addition to this obvious idea of pleasure, reading to children has certain other advantages. It has spontaneity. A story may begin or end the day. It can be used as part of "reading group," or it can be a quiet activity after lunch or recess. Reading aloud does not require a response from the children, other than perhaps a chuckle or an expression of sympathy. They need only listen and enjoy. Research supports reading aloud to children. In a study of primary grade children, Cohen (1968) found improved vocabulary and reading achievement scores when pupils were exposed to stories read aloud by the teacher. In logitudinal investigations of young children, Durkin (1966) found that early readers had been read to from the age of three or before. There are currently books available that have been expressly published for children as young as infants.

Books for reading aloud are generally highly accessible. They are available from the school library, public library, and paperback book clubs. Children enjoy hearing their old favorites from the classroom collection again and again. After they have begun to form the "book habit," students will bring books from home they want the teacher to read, or that they want to share with the class themselves. It is that habit of choosing a book to read, either independently or to others, that should be encouraged.

Children's literature offers a wide variety of content to reading instruction. Books provide experiences needed to broaden the child's background and to enhance language development. Many children receive little exposure to people and activities outside their own neighborhoods or communities. The use of a wealth of children's books in the classroom brings to children customs and cultures of other people, an historical perspective to their own culture, an imaginative look into the future and to "worlds beyond," a glimpse at fantasy, and information about their own environment. It is the responsibility of the teacher to provide these vicarious experiences to supplement the child's background.

All children come to school with language. They have not, however, all had the same opportunities to use language. The scope of basal readers tends to be limited by vocabulary controls and readability levels. Children's books not only offer extensive vocabulary but also a variety of language patterns. In a study of the language acquisition of children between the ages of six and ten, Chomsky (1972) found a positive correlation between stages of linguistic development and exposure to literature, as determined by an inventory of their previous experiences. Language-in-literature activities invite children to compare and contrast the expository style of informational books, the imaginative descriptions in fantasy and science fiction, verbal humor in humorous selections, and the musical language of poetry. Exposure to these various types of language can help children build their reading, writing, and speaking vocabularies.

Literature allows children the opportunity to think critically. Stories in basal readers provide for extensive literal level comprehension but instances requiring children to think beyond that level are limited. With teacher guidance, the variety of content in books offers children chances to infer meanings, make judgments and assess values, compare characters and settings, and determine various authors' styles. Research indicates that children expect a story to be structured (Guthrie, 1977). Knowledge of story structure assists in the comprehension and recall of a story. Heavy exposure to a variety of literature aids in the development of such knowledge. Children's books can also serve as bases for developing taste in literature. Although taste is something that cannot be "taught" to children, its development may be assisted by providing a wide variety of literary models in an atmosphere in which a child may sample them. Literature is also an excellent stimulus for children to do creative writing of their own.

Children's literature also serves a personal function. It can help children acquire a better understanding of society and human behavior. Current societal topics of interest, such as the elderly, death, divorce, alcoholism, drug use, exceptional children, women's roles, and ethnic awareness, are reflected in the literature for children today. Sutherland, Monson, and Arbuthnot (1981) discussed children's literature in terms of satisfying needs, such as physical well-being, to love and be loved, to belong, to achieve, to know, for change, and for beauty and order. Most importantly, children need good books.

In summary, the use of children's books in the classroom has the obvious educational advantages of assisting language development, broadening experiential background, encouraging children to think critically and write creatively, and expanding upon the basal reading program. The use of children's literature has the personal advantages of helping to satisfy emotional needs and to increase the child's awareness of society. Of primary importance, a positive attitude toward children's books at an early age tends to lead to a lifelong appreciation of good literature and reading. As Huck (1979) stated, "Delight in books only comes about through long and loving experiences with them" (p. 704).

Values of Learning Centers

Centers organize learning experiences for students by allowing choice within a framework of structure. Learning centers offer an alternative in classroom management to the traditional seatwork activities. Centers are usually popular with children because they make students active participants in their learning. With centers, children may choose from a variety of interesting activities. This element of choice encourages self-reliance on the part of the students. They are expected to operate independently within the learning center framework.

The use of centers also improves social interaction among the children. Because of the independent nature of many activities, children must engage in self-discipline. Further, they must modify their behavior to fit a classroom environment in which others are pursuing individual interests. In addition, many of the activities can be structured for partners or for small group work. Purposeful shared activity can increase social interaction.

Learning centers provide a viable way of individualizing instruction. Students have different learning styles as well as different interests. With the variety of activities in centers, children can choose those that best fit their preferred mode of learning and that satisfy their interests. Learning centers can meet individual instructional needs of students as well. Centers are usually organized with a specific set of objectives in mind, and the activities are designed to fulfill those objectives. The additional practice offered by these activities can help overcome individual difficulties of students. Learning center instruction may be further individualized in that every student need not be required to complete every activity in a specific center.

The components of a learning center can be quite varied. Skills work in the form of games and worksheets, art activities, listening activities, creative writing, and independent reading are some possibilities for a center. Active involvement of the students is an important consideration planning center activities. Variety is limited only by the imagination of the teacher and students.

Another important factor to consider in the planning of learning centers is cost. Center components can be made from quite inexpensive materials. The centers suggested in this book are not costly to construct and can be made with materials found in the home or community.

In summary, learning centers can serve as a means for moving students away from learning experiences that are totally directed by the teacher and toward learning activities in which students have been involved in the decision making.

REFERENCES

Chomsky, Carol. "Stages in Language Development and Reading Exposure." *Harvard Educational Review* 42 (1972): 1 - 33.

Cohen, Dorothy, "The Effect of Literature on Vocabulary and Reading Achievement." *Elementary English* 45 (1968): 209 - 213.

Durkin, Dolores. "The Achievement of Pre-School Readers: Two Longitudinal Studies." *Reading Research Quarterly* 1 (1966): 5 - 36.

Guthrie, John. "Story Comprehension." *The Reading Teacher* 30 (1977): 574 - 77.

Huck, Charlotte. *Children's Literature in the Elementary School*. 3rd ed. updated. New York: Holt, Rinehart and Winston, 1979.

Sutherland, Zena, Monson, Dianne and Arbuthnot, May Hill. *Children and Books*. 6th ed. Glenview, Ill.: Scott Foresman, 1981.

CHAPTER TWO

How To
Construct, Manage
And Evaluate
Learning Centers

Construction

The construction of a learning center should be carefully considered and well-planned in advance. Designing and planning can save many hours of work and can enable one to avoid mistakes that waste time and supplies.

The initial consideration should be the available space and adaptability of the classroom. Center areas or bases should be designed so they can be used for a variety of centers in succession and, if possible, so they can provide storage. Teachers can accomplish this goal in a variety of ways.

Teachers who have enough space may purchase a cardboard house at relatively little expense, and use it as the base for their center as well as storage for materials. Activities can be attached to the sides of the house with hooks or brads, pockets made of oilcloth can be attached to the house, and materials can be placed in boxes and arranged around the house. The house itself can be used for storage or for a quiet place for children to read, write or work activities. An old piece of rug or carpet squares, some cushions, and posters or pictures make it an inviting space.

A treehouse also makes an exciting center. A sturdy platform with adequate railings can be constructed and this platform provides an enticing work or reading area. The space beneath the platform can serve as the center area and also provide storage space.

Wardrobe boxes purchased at a moving company or refrigeration boxes can provide adequate center bases. Again, activities can be affixed to the base with L hooks, cup hooks, brads, oilcloth pockets, etc. A magnetic board can be attached to one side of the sturdy box by taking an appropriately sized piece of sheet metal, drilling holes in the four corners and fastening it to the box with wing bolts. A flannel board could also be made by cutting a piece of cardboard the desired size, covering it with flannel, and attaching it to the cardboard box with brads.

Stores dispose of display stands when the merchandise is sold, or when the ad campaign is over, or on a rotating basis. Instead of having a great center base thrown away, ask the manager to call when it is to be discarded. Centers have been made of L'Eggs display racks, fancy fruit display cartons, paperback book racks, and the like.

Providing a sense of privacy can be important in a classroom, yet the teacher needs to be able to supervise all classroom activities. This privacy can be accomplished in several ways with centers. Using pegboard and hinges, a divider can be constructed of any size desired. The base is completely flexible in use, as shelves can easily be placed on the pegboard, and hooks and pockets can be located at will.

Privacy can also be achieved by rearranging furniture and creating centers by pulling bookcases away from walls, using the backs as well as the shelves to display items, and using objects such as a free-standing abacus or a chart stand to help create an area.

Another device is to make hanging dividers by attaching burlap to a dowel rod and hanging them from the ceiling. Activities and/or pockets can be attached to the burlap with yarn and changed whenever necessary. The splashes of color also add to the attractiveness of the room.

A center can be organized around a bulletin board. Activities can be placed on the board and on the floor under the board, and stations can be located in other parts of the room.

Center construction ideas are limited only by one's imagination. Centers have been created around and on a stepladder, on two coatracks with bamboo poles hung between them, and in a suitcase by a teacher of the homebound. Imaginative teachers may further elaborate on the ideas presented here.

Another concern in center construction is durability. Time and money should not be wasted, so all materials should be as sturdy as possible and protected when feasible.

Containers for activities should be durable to begin with. Strong cardboard containers should be used and the corners reinforced. Zip-loc bags are strong and transparent and they can be easily labeled with masking tape and pen; heavy brown envelopes are better than flimsy ones; and tag board rather than construction paper, which will fade, tear and become brittle, should be used.

Game boards should be constructed so that more than one game can be played on them. They should be attractive and covered with clear contact paper or laminated. Water-based markers should be used to draw on the game board, as other markers will "bleed" in time, and crayons will run when laminated. If photo album corners are used to hold cards on a game board, the corners should be put on the board, covered with clear contact paper, and the contact paper slit with a razor blade where each corner is. This procedure will keep the corners from popping off.

Markers or game pieces for games should be attractive but not items children will be tempted to keep. Little cars on wheels are cute, but if the board is bumped they roll and then there is a problem with where each player was on the board. Bottle caps, fancy buttons, small sea shells, and the like make good game pieces.

Dice should be made, not purchased. A die may be made by cutting an appropriately sized square from a sponge. Mark on the six sides of the die with a marker. Use numerals or dots and mark 1, 2, 3, 1, 2, 3, on the six sides. By allowing a player a maximum of only three moves, the players have more opportunities to practice the skills in the game and the game lasts longer. The use of sponge dice also keeps the noise level at a minimum.

A spinner can be constructed by cutting a 4-inch square of cardboard and drawing a circle in the center. Divide the circle into the number of digits desired. Make an arrow of tagboard or poster board and fasten it in the center of the circle with a brass fastener. It is best to use a hole punch to make the holes in the arrow and the circle, which will allow freer movement of the arrow. If the arrow fits too tightly, the spinner will not spin. A flat metal washer inserted between the arrow and the circle will also help the spinner move more easily. The child can spin the arrow by holding a corner of the cardboard and snapping the arrow with his/her finger.

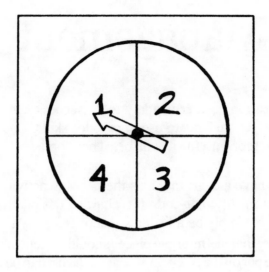

Materials used in centers should be as inexpensive as possible. Send home a list of materials for parents to save and send in periodically. It is better to gather materials all year and have them on hand when needed. A sample list of materials might include the following:

cardboard boxes — all sizes
shoe boxes
cereal boxes
wood and hinges
pegboard and hooks
window shades
oil cloth
burlap
old rugs and carpet squares
contact paper
pizza rounds
library pockets
clothespins
yarn

shower curtain rings
cup hooks
butter tubs (plastic)
Pringles cans
McDonald's styrofoam containers
styrofoam meat trays
zip-loc bags –– all sizes
wallpaper scraps or books
magnets
string or cord
magazines
catalogs
tin cans — assorted sizes
cloth scraps

Management

Management of a learning center is a key to its success. Centers are meant to help teachers provide activities for students to use to practice skills. The less the teacher has to supervise the center, the more useful it will be. Therefore, good advanced planning is necessary.

Each center should have a chart that lists the possible activities in the center. If you believe it necessary, you might color-code the chart to designate activities for different groups. Or, the chart might simply be a listing so recordkeeping is made easier.

Each game or activity that has multiple pieces should be kept in a separate container. A list of the pieces should be put on the box or container. The list can be done with color-coding for nonreaders or words for readers.

For example:

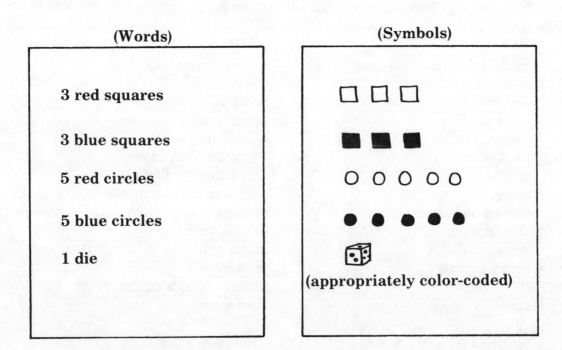

(Words)	(Symbols)
3 red squares	
3 blue squares	
5 red circles	
5 blue circles	
1 die	
	(appropriately color-coded)

Containers should also be carefully constructed to reduce noise and confusion. For example, if a Spill and Spell type game is used, it could become noisy and could also be a temptation to toss the cubes wildly. If the container is designed carefully, these potential problems can be controlled. Take a cardbord box of suitable dimensions and line it with felt. Students are to toss the cubes in the lined box. Use of the box reduces both noise and the area in which the cubes can be thrown. If students break the rules, they may not play the game for a designated amount of time.

Rules should be clearly and carefully provided for each activity. If the activity is a game, a rule book could be provided or the rules could be written on the lid of the box. Tapes could be made for nonreaders. If the rules are simple, the teacher can go through the activity with small groups of students so they will understand how to play.

Rules for center use should be simple, few in number and strictly enforced. A few basic rules will be more effective than numerous insignificant ones that students are bound to break. Rules should fit the center. For example, one room with a treehouse had the rule: "no spitting." One can readily understand the temptation a child might feel when lying on his or her stomach and looking down on a vulnerable head! In this case, the penalty for breaking the rule was no treehouse for a week. Rules should include putting away all materials and cleaning up the center when finished.

Centers are usually limited in the number of students who can participate at one time. Some activities can be designed so they can be taken to another area to complete. Others must be completed within the center. Various methods can be used to control center participation.

Students can be assigned to work in the centers on specific days or at specific times. Certain centers, such as a listening station, are easily limited by the number of headphones available. Number limits can be set such as with a rule that no more than three people can work in an area at a time. One teacher made a pegboard divider and painted a train engine on it. She placed four engineer's caps on hooks. When a student worked in the center, he/she wore a cap. If there were no caps available, a child knew he or she couldn't work in the center. Another idea is to construct a chart for the center that lists each activity with a pocket envelope beside it. An appropriate number of colored slips put in each pocket will indicate how many children can do that activity at one time. As a student chooses the activity, he/she removes the matching slip and returns it when finished. An empty pocket signals a student to choose another activity.

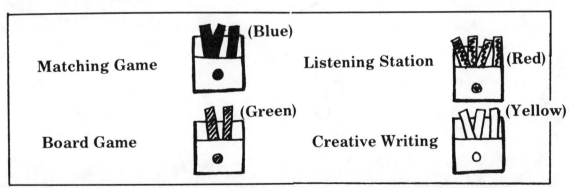

The use of some activities might be limited with a timer to give more students the opportunity to participate. Students might also use a magic slate to "sign up" to use an activity next. The slate is easily erased when filled.

Assignment of a weekly center monitor who has responsibility for seeing the center is organized at the end of each day can save the teacher time and effort.

Evaluation

Self-evaluation is the primary goals of learning centers. The purpose is to reinforce concepts and to extend learning, not to provide a basis for grading. If a student learns by reading the answers the first time or two, that is fine. If the student can eventually complete the activity independently, then he/she has learned.

An answer key or answer booklet can be provided with the game or activity. In some games, one player might be designated the "judge" to use the answer book and determine the correctness of the responses.

The answer key might be made part of the game or activity for self-checking by a single player. It could be glued to the game, or the answers could be placed on the back.

For example:

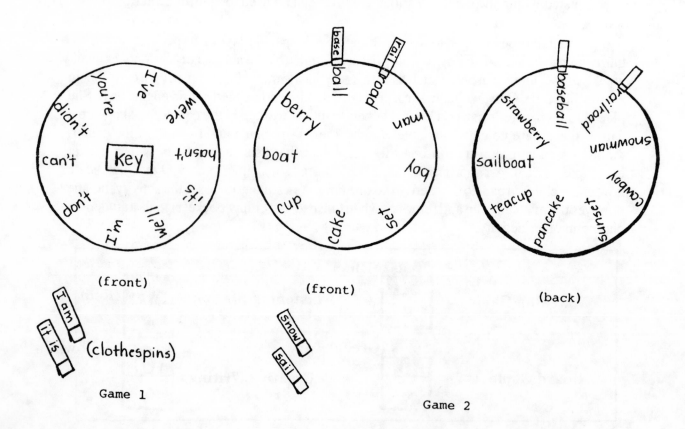

(front)

(clothespins)

Game 1

(front)

Game 2

(back)

16

Color coding or symbol coding could be used. In a classification activity, for example, answers could be shown in the following manner:

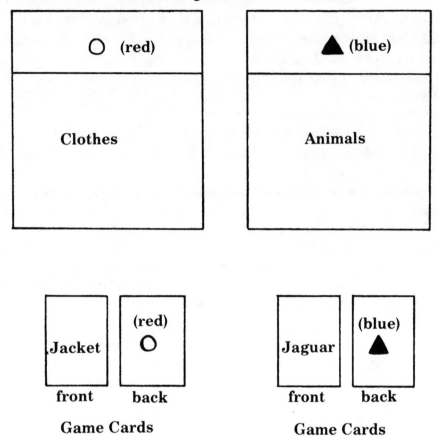

Game Cards   Game Cards

An additional and more sophisticated method would be to use an electric light board, as described on pages 18-21.

The final evaluation is whether students are attracted to the center, make use of it, and learn from it. There must be an adequate payoff for the time and effort expended to create the center. One way of ensuring that this payoff occurs is to create purposeful, carefully developed centers. Another is to change centers frequently enough to maintain interest and learning. Centers should be rotated every few weeks. It is better to have students wishing they could do more than to have them bored with the task at hand.

Directions for making Electric Light Board*

Materials Needed·

    wood (pine is recommended)

        1 piece cut 1" x 12" x 18" (if plywood is used, ¾" thickness is better)

        2 pieces cut 1" x 4" x 18"

        2 pieces cut 1" x 4" x 10½"

These materials may be purchased at a hardware store:

    34 brads (cup hooks may be used)

    16 — #6 - 32 x 1¼" machine screws with nuts

24 — #6 - flat washers
2 — #6 x ½" wood screws

These materials may be purchased at an electronic supply store (such as Radio Shack):

1 — #222 light bulb
1 — lamp socket for #222 light bulb
1 — battery holder for 2 'D' cell batteries
2 — 'D' cell batteries
1 pair probes (volt meter test leads)
8 — 18" long "alligator clip" jumper leads

Constructing the light board:

Cut wood to dimensions indicated.

On front of the board, mark locations for match-up screws, light, and brads (see front view drawing).

Drill ⅛" holes for match-up screws. Drill hole for lamp socket.

Stain or paint wood as desired.

When dry, nail or screw the side boards to the front board.

Insert #6 - 32 x 1¼" machine screws (match-up screws). Place one flat washer and one nut on 1R and tighten the nut. Repeat for 2R through 8R.

Wire match-ups on back as follows:

Cut one of the jumper leads so that it is 15" long. Strip ¾" of insulation from the cut end and bend the bare wire to form a "hook." Place the "hook" between the flat washers of 1L and tighten the nut as shown below. Repeat this procedure for the remaining seven jumper leads, using the following table as a guide:

Position	Length
2L	13½"
3L	12"
4L	10½"
5L	10½"
6L	12"
7L	13½"
8L	15"

The other ends of the jumper leads are clipped onto the 1R-8R screws to achieve the desired match-up code. The match-up codes can then be changed very easily to insure that the children do not memorize a pattern of responses.

Insert and secure lamp socket.

Drill 1/16" pilot holes and secure battery holder using two #6 - 32 wood screws (see back view drawing).

Cut probes to desired length. File points of probe tips so they are not sharp. Drill two ⅛" holes in the bottom side board. Insert the red probe wire cut end through one of the ⅛" holes and the black probe wire through the other hole. Ensuring that there is ample length to reach

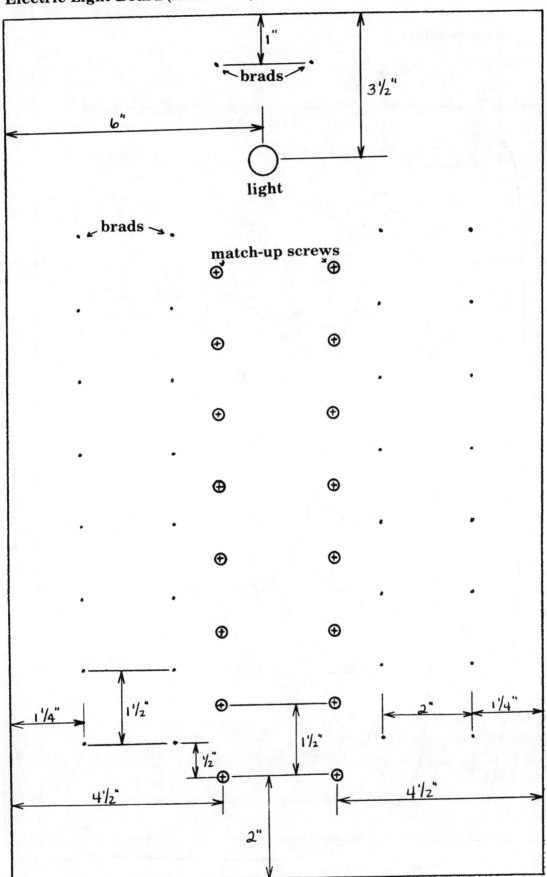

Electric Light Board (back view)

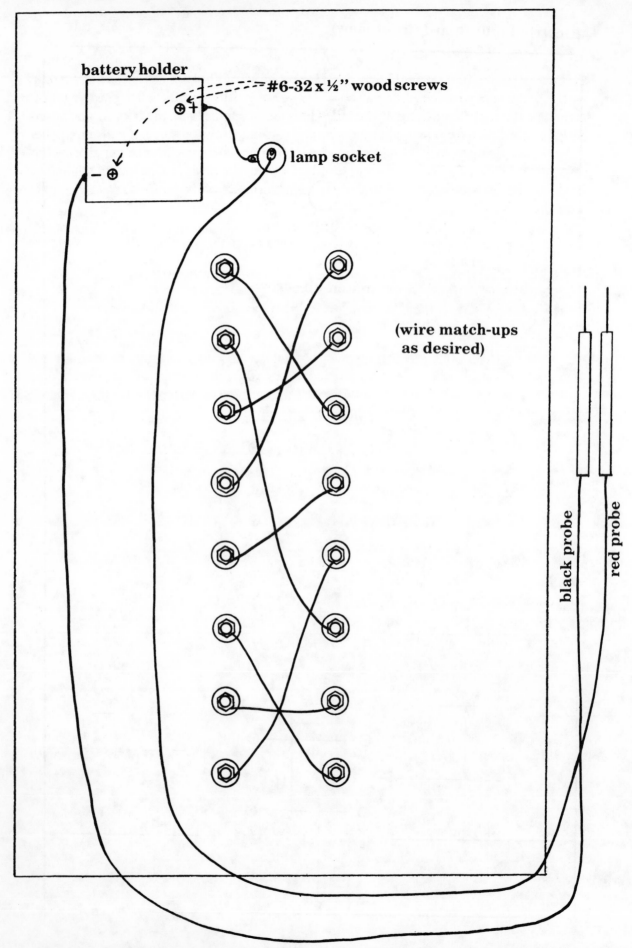

battery holder

#6-32 x ½" wood screws

lamp socket

(wire match-ups as desired)

black probe

red probe

the battery holder, tie a simple knot in the black probe wire. The knot will act as a strain relief for the probe wire when children pull on it. Tie a knot in the red probe wire. The two probes should be of nearly equal length when the knots are in contact with the bottom side board. Strip ¼" insulation from the red probe wire and solder it to one terminal of the lamp socket. Strip ¼" insulation from the black probe wire and solder it to the negative terminal of the battery holder. Solder one end of a short length of wire to the positive terminal of the battery holder and solder the other end to the remaining terminal of the lamp socket. (See back view drawing).

Screw light bulb into lamp socket. Place "D" cell batteries into battery holder. Test operation by touching probe tips to known match-up. The bulb should light up.

Attach brads.

* *Special thanks to Tom Wendelin for the design of this board.*

Electric Board Cards

Multiple sets of cards can be made so that the electric board may be used for any matching-type game. Hang the title card and match cards on the brads. When the children touch the match-up screws with a correct match, the light will go on for self-checking. Change match-up patterns frequently. Matching card (actual size):

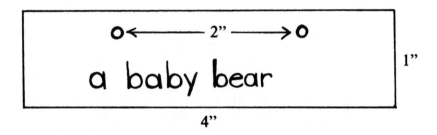

Title card should be 6" x 1¾" in size.

CHAPTER THREE

Folklore

The folklore center includes activities for folk tales, fables, and pourquoi tales ("why" stories).

The backdrop of the center is a large bridge from "The Three Billy Goats Gruff." Cardboard or heavy brown paper taped to the wall may serve as the bridge. Have the children make a troll to put under the bridge. These "troll" books may help them with ideas:

d'Aulaire, Ingri and Edgar. *D'Aulaires' Trolls*. Doubleday, 1972.

dePaola, Tomie. *Helga's Dowry*. Harcourt, 1977.

Marshall, Edward. *Troll Country*. Il. By James Marshall. Dial, 1980.

Sharmat, Marjorie W. *The Trolls of Twelfth Street*. Il. by Ben Shecter. Coward, 1979.

The troll may be drawn on large paper, or it may be made three dimensional by stuffing a grocery bag and adding features for the head, and by stuffing old clothes for the body. A few bushes and stones will complete the backdrop.

25

Folk and Fairy Tales

FOLKLORE   Creative Writing

The theme of the creative writing station in the folklore center is "Jack and the Beanstalk."

1) Give the children story suggestions. For variety, use these ideas to change the station:

a. The giant's bags of gold. Put pictures or introductory sentences on "gold" coins (paper) in drawstring bags for story starters.

b. The magic harp. Use different types of music on cassette tapes as a stimulus for creative writing. (Provide appropriate verbal introduction to the musical selection.)

c. The hen that laid the golden eggs. Paint L'eggs containers gold; put ideas for stories on slips of paper or small objects inside. Sample arrangement:

1. **Take one of the giant's golden eggs.**
2. **Look inside the egg.**
3. **Write a story about what you find there.**

Hen may be a cardboard cut-out or a calico hen like the popular crafts item.

2) Suggestions for creative stories based on folk tales:

a. If a fairy gave you three wishes, what would you wish for and why would you wish for those things?

b. You know how to make "stone soup." Write your own recipe for something you like.

c. You are the giant's wife. Convince the giant that he should *not* eat Jack.

d. Write a folk tale and illustrate it.

e. Write a newspaper story about the capture of the wolf in "Little Red Riding Hood."

f. You are the *eigth* dwarf. Tell your name and describe yourself.

g. If you had a magic lamp like Aladdin's, tell about your genie and what you would have him do for you.

h. Pick a folk tale character and write his/her life story. (For example, the wicked queen or Snow White).

i. If you were the size of Tom Thumb or Thumbelina, write a story about the kinds of problems you would have at home and at school.

j. What if your hair started growing and wouldn't stop until it was *longer* that Rapunzel's! Write a story about yourself.

3) Display finished products on a large beanstalk.

Beanstalk may be suspended from the ceiling or taped to the wall.

"You Can't Catch Me" is a game involving story content in folk tales. It can be played at all levels of the primary grades by changing the difficulty of the match cards. For example, the cards could match:

    1) a picture of a character and an object associated with that character

    2) a picture of a character and his/her name

    3) a picture of a character or object and the title of the folk tale

    4) a quotation from a character's speech and a picture of the character

    5) a quotation and the title of the folk tale

By going from simple to more complex tasks, the match cards can be adapted to the ability levels of the children.

Directions for playing:

Two to four players may play. Match cards should be of two different colors. The first player draws a card of each color. If he/she makes a match, the player lays down the pair and chooses a *game card* which tells how to move on the game board. If a match is not made, the player returns one card to the stack and the next player takes a turn. One color of the match cards should be designated as the one to be returned. (For example, if blue and yellow cards are used, players might return a blue card every time and keep the yellow card.) All cards should be coded on the back so players may check that they have made a correct match. The game proceeds until one player has reached the end of the path.

Vary the types of moves which the game cards direct the child to make. Directions of the game cards should reflect the gingerbread man theme of the game. Some suggestions for game cards are:

    1) The fox is taking a nap. Sneak ahead two spaces.

    2) A hungry little boy is just ahead and ready to eat you! Hide behind the nearest rock and stay on your space.

    3) You just fell into a stream. Go back to beginning and dry out.

    4) The fox is getting close. Climb the nearest tree and stay on your space.

    5) The fox has set a trap ahead. Go back 2 spaces and take the long way around.

    6) Run, run, run, as fast as you can to the next space.

Add other game cards of this type.

"I'll grind his bones to make my bread."

The giant

GAME CARDS

Run, run, run as fast as you can to the next space.

You CAN'T CATCH ME!

Use this as a model for a large gameboard.

(brown felt with features of yarn or fabric trim)

Match Cards

1	2

Game Cards

30

"Catch and Attach" involves attaching prefixes and suffixes to the base words on the game board to make new words. Prepare a set of cards with these prefixes and suffixes on them:

-ly	-less	re-
-en	-er	pre-
-ness	-able	un-
-full	-es	dis-

You may substitute base words other than the ones suggested on your game board. Directions for playing:

Two to four children may play. Have a supply of game pieces available in four colors, and let each player choose a color for the game. The first player draws a prefix/suffix card. If he/she can form a word by adding the prefix or suffix to the base word in the first space, that player gets to claim the space with one of his/her markers. If it is not possible to form a word, the card is returned to the bottom of the deck and the next player draws. When all cards have been drawn, the game is finished. The player who has claimed the most spaces is the winner. An answer key with all possible new words should be provided for checking in case of questions.

SAMPLE GAME CARD

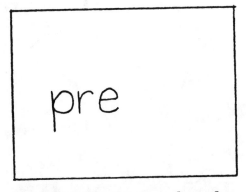

Use the sample gameboard on the next page as a model for a large board.

31

CATCH AND ATTACH

Spin to see who goes first.

GAME CARD

32

Put the words below in alpha-betical order.

Use this space to make a genie coming out of the lamp.

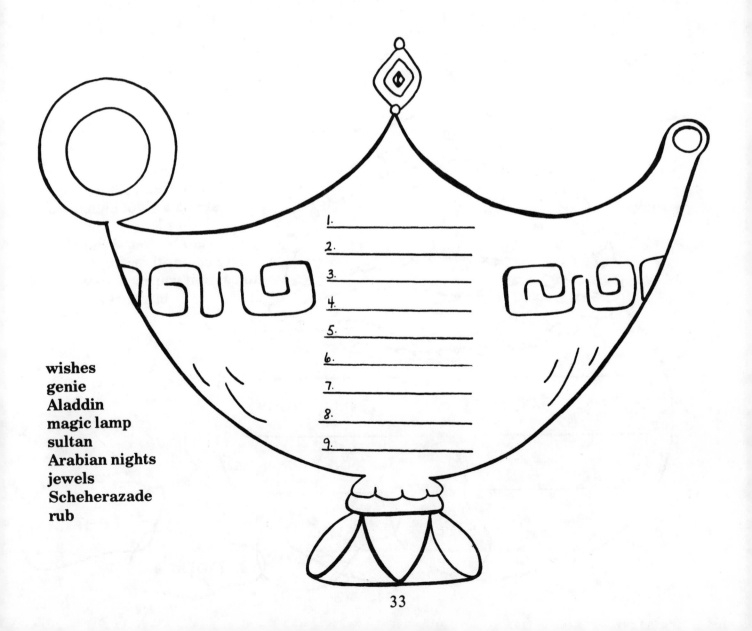

1. _____
2. _____
3. _____
4. _____
5. _____
6. _____
7. _____
8. _____
9. _____

wishes
genie
Aladdin
magic lamp
sultan
Arabian nights
jewels
Scheherazade
rub

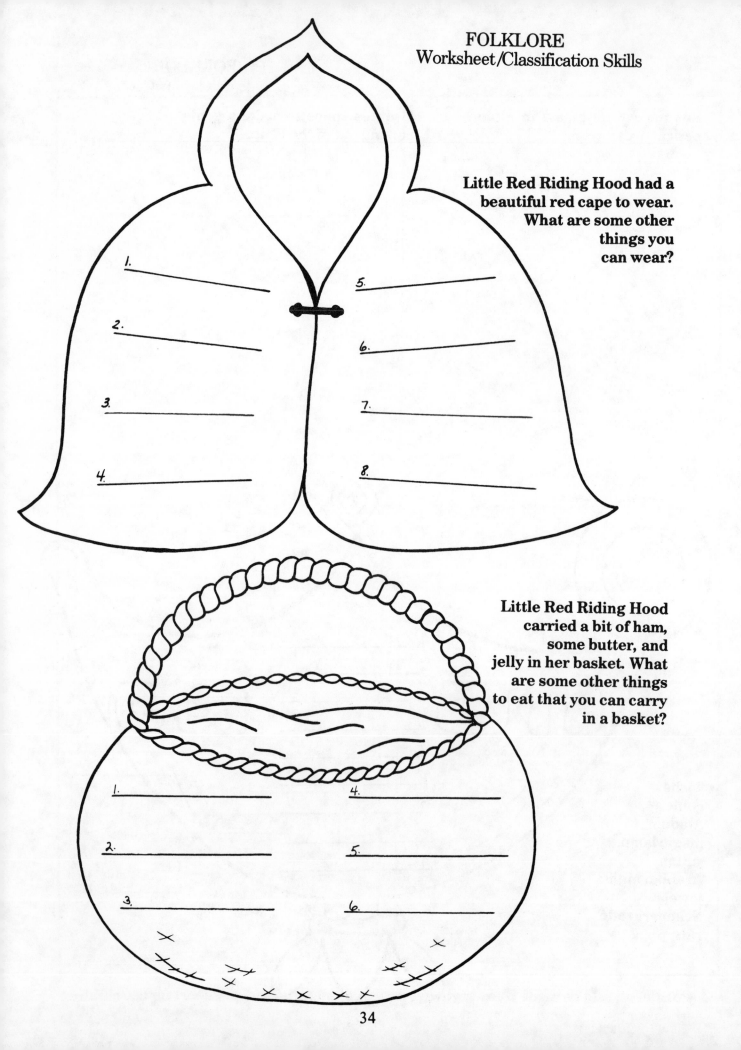

Little Red Riding Hood had a beautiful red cape to wear. What are some other things you can wear?

1. _____
2. _____
3. _____
4. _____
5. _____
6. _____
7. _____
8. _____

Little Red Riding Hood carried a bit of ham, some butter, and jelly in her basket. What are some other things to eat that you can carry in a basket?

1. _____
2. _____
3. _____
4. _____
5. _____
6. _____

34

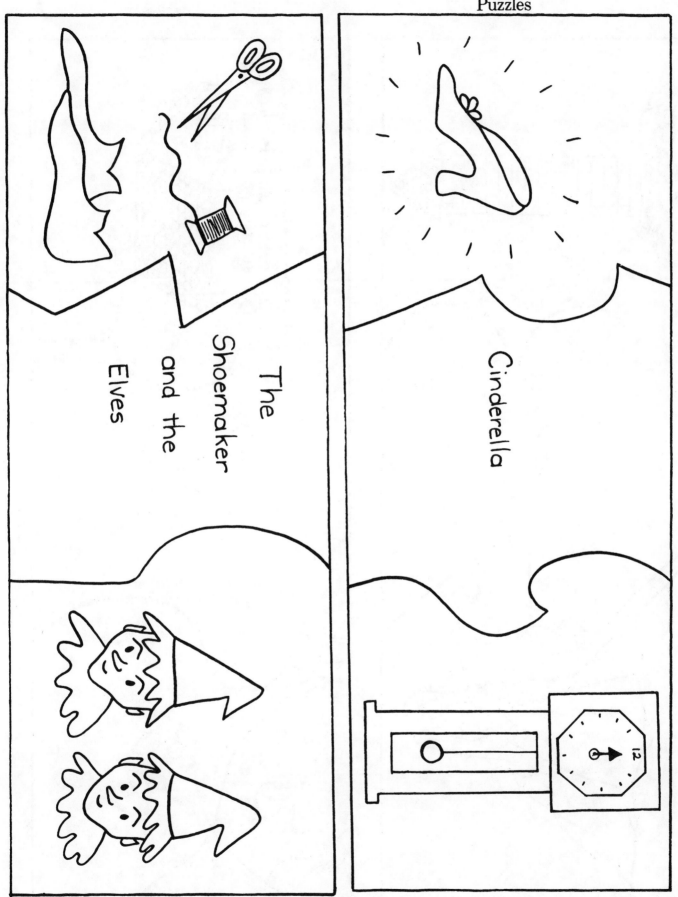

The
Shoemaker
and the
Elves

Cinderella

Puzzles should be made from tagboard or similar material and cut apart for the children to assemble.

35

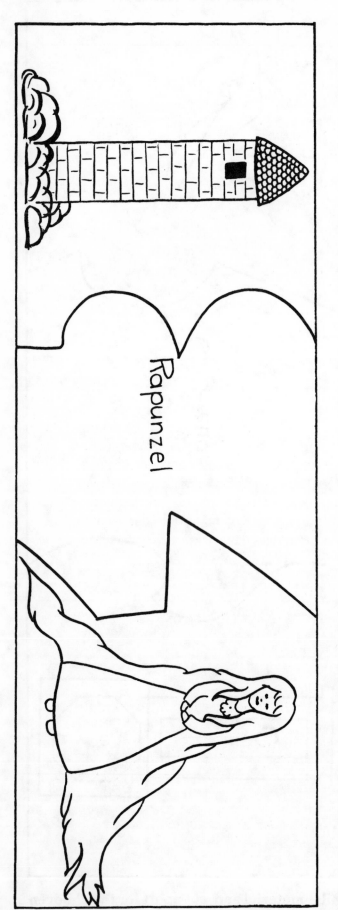

Rapunzel

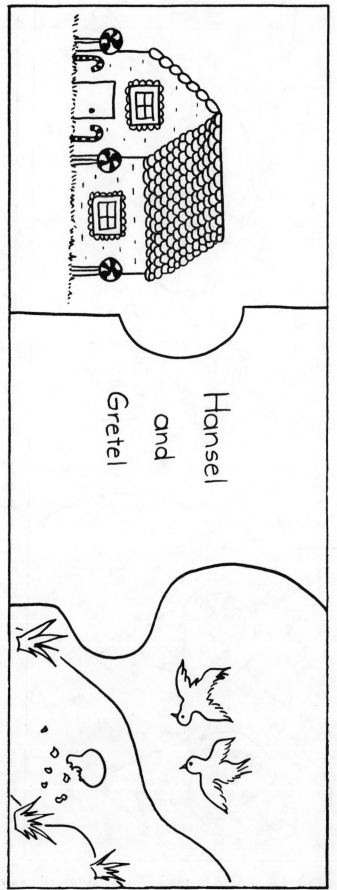

Hansel
and
Gretel

36

Comparing Folk Tales

FOLKLORE   Critical Reading

All countries have folk tales as part of their culture. Many of these tales are basically alike, with only names changed from country to country. For example, Rumpelstiltskin is very well known to our children, but he also appears in the tales of other countries. Shown above are three versions of a Rumpelstiltskin tale. Have students locate these books and compare the parts of the tale (beginnings, endings, tasks the person must do, how the person discovers Rumplestiltskin's name, etc.) and illustrations. Then they could write and/or illustrate their own versions.

Grimm. *Rumplelstiltskin.* Il. by Jacqueline Ayer. Harcourt, 1967.

Ness, Evaline. *Tom Tit Tot.* Scribner, 1965.

Grimm. *Rumpelstiltskin.* Il. By William Stobbs. Walck, 1970.

Grimm. *Rumpelstiltskin.* Retold by Edith Tarcov. Il. by Edward Gorey. Four Winds, 1973.

Zemach, Harve. *Duffy and the Devil.* Il. by Margot Zemach. Farrar, 1973.

Rumpelstiltskin. Filmstrip and record from Miller-Brody Productions.

English Folk and Fairy Tales including *Tom Tit Tot.* Cassettes from Miller-Brody Productions.

Below are other tales that have been adapted and illustrated by various authors. Use these as a beginning, but see how many others your students can find.

Anglund, Joan Walsh. *Nibble, Nibble Mousekin.* Harcourt, 1962.

Grimm. *Hansel and Gretel.* Il. By Warren Chappell. Knopf, 1944.

_____. *Hansel and Gretel.* Il. by Arnold Lobel. Delacorte, 1971.

_____. *Hansel and Gretel.* Il. By Celine Leopold. Walck, 1970.

_____. *Hansel and Gretel*. Retold by Ruth Belov Gross. Il. By Margot Tomes. Scholastic, 1974.

_____. *Hansel and Gretel*. Translated by Charles Scribner, Jr. Il. by Adrienne Adams. Scribner, 1975.

_____. *Hansel and Gretel*. Translated by Elizabeth D. Crawford. Il. by Lisbeth Zwerger. Morrow, 1980.

_____. *Hansel and Gretel*. Il. by Susan Jeffers. Dial, 1980.

* *

Cohen, Barbara. *Lovely Vassilisa*. Il. By Anatoly Ivanov. Atheneum, 1980.

Galdone, Paul, (Ret. and Il.) *Cinderella*. McGraw-Hill, 1978.

Hogrogian, Nonny, (Il.). *Cinderella*. Greenwillow, 1981.

Le Cain, Errol, (Trans. and Il.). *Cinderella*. Bradbury, 1972.

Louie, Ai-ling, (Ret.). *Yeh Shen*. Il. by Ed Young. Philomel, 1982.

Montresor, Beni, (Il.). *Cinderella*. Knopf, 1965.

Perrault, Charles. *Cinderella*. Trans. and Il. by Marcia Brown. Scribner, 1954.

Steele, Flora A. *Tattercoats*. Il. by Diane Goode. Bradbury, 1976.

* *

Grimm. *The Sleeping Beauty*. Il. By Feliz Hoffman. Harcourt, 1959.

_____. *The Sleeping Beauty*. Adapted and Il. by Trina Schart Hyman. Little, Brown, 1974.

_____. *Thorn Rose or the Sleeping Beauty*. Il. by Errol Le Cain. Bradbury, 1975.

_____. *The Sleeping Beauty*. Il. By David Walker. Crowell, 1976.

_____. *The Sleeping Beauty*. Retold and Il. by Warwick Hutton. Atheneum, 1979.

Fables

Fables are short tales which attempt to teach some type of lesson. The moral is usually directly stated but may be implied. Characters in fables are primarily animals that speak and take on human characteristics. Although the majority of primary children will have difficulty comprehending the moral lessons. there are many well-illustrated versions of fables that they can listen to and enjoy.

After the children have heard a number of the more familiar fables, they may follow-up with the activity on fable characters illustrated below.

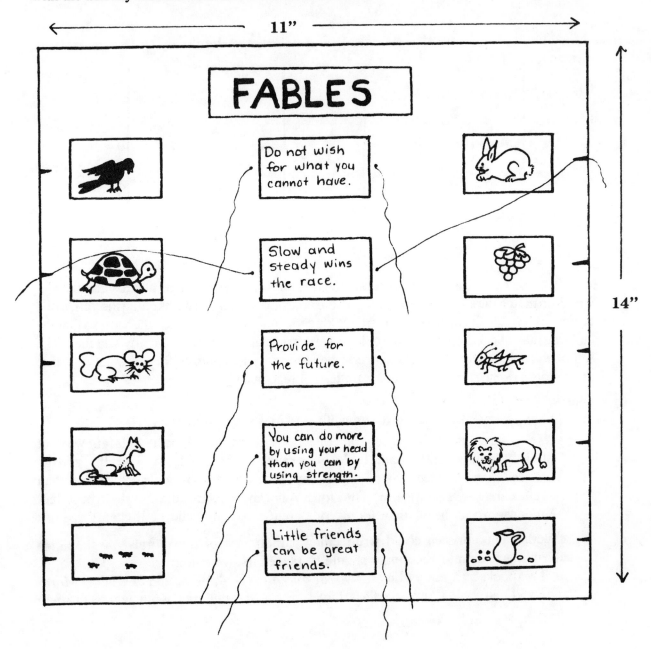

Directions for making:

The board should be made from cardboard or heavy weight poster board. Picture cards and word cards should not permanently attached to the board so that different fables may be substituted. Pieces of Velcro may be used to attach cards to the board. Use different colors of yarn. Punch a hole on either side of the center card, and thread the yarn behind the board as shown:

front   **back**

color code dot

Cut notches in the cardboard along the outside edges where picture cards are located. Children match the animal characters with the appropriate moral by stretching the yarn to the correct notch. On the back of the board, color code the notches to match the yarn so that the children may check their work. The color code dots should not be permanently attached. The self-check color code should be changed when the cards are changed for a new game so that the children do not memorize a *color* pattern of responses.

Activities for high ability students:

1) Set up a creative writing station with activities such as these:

a. Have the children look at several collections of fables and locate different ways of stating the morals from the same fable. For example, the moral from "The Hare and the Tortoise" may be stated, "Steady going wins the race" or Slow and sure is better than fast and careless." Likewise, in "The North Wind and the Sun," the moral can be stated, "Kindness works better than force" or "Gentleness may succeed when force has

failed." The children could write other paraphrases of the morals. A simplified thesaurus and junior dictionary should be placed in the station.

b. Two books by Mercer Mayer, *Two Moral Tales* (Dial, 1974) and *Two More Moral Tales* (Dial, 1975), are wordless fables. Have the children write words to these fables.

c. Prepare a set of cards with animal names written on them and another set of cards with moral lessons written on them. Have the children draw two animal cards and one moral card and write a fable. For example, one might draw a hippopotamus and a parakeet as characters and the moral, "Never trust a flatterer." Have available the book *Fables* by Arnold Lobel (Harper, 1980), a collection of original fables featuring a variety of animal characters, for the children to read.

2) To further develop the critical reading skills of the students, have them read modern fables and compare them with traditional fables, noting similarities of characters' behaviors and moral lessons. For example, children might find many similarities between Steig's *Amos and Boris* and "The Lion and the Mouse." *Frederick* by Leo Lionni and "The Ant and the Grasshopper" may also be compared. Students might also compare traditional fables with the "twisted" morals in *Fables You Shouldn't Pay Any Attention To* by Florence Parry Heide and Sylvia Van Clief (Lippincott, 1978).

Modern fables:

Ciardi, John. *John J. Plenty and Fiddler Dan*. Il. By Madeleine Gekiere. Lippin-
    cott, 1963.
Lionni, Leo. *Tico and the Golden Wings*. Pantheon, 1964.
_____. *Frederick*. Pantheon, 1967.
_____. *Biggest House in the World*. Pantheon, 1968.
_____. *Fish is Fish*. Pantheon, 1970.
_____. *Pezzettino*. Pantheon, 1975.
Steig, William. *Amos and Boris*. Farrar, 1971.

SELECTED BIBLIOGRAPHY OF TRADITIONAL FABLES

Artzybasheff, Boris (Ed. and Il.). *Aesop's Fables*. Viking, 1933.
Brown, Marcia. *Once a Mouse*. Scribner's, 1961.
Calhoun, Mary. *Old Man Whickutt's Donkey*. Il. By Tomie de Paola. Parent's, 1975.
Carle, Eric (Adap. and Il.). *Twelve Tales from Aesop*. Philomel, 1980.
Chapman, Gaynor (Il.). *Aesop's Fables*. Atheneum, 1971.
Cooney, Barbara (Ed. and Il.). *Chanticleer and the Fox*. Crowell, 1958.
Galdone, Paul (Il.) *The Monkey and the Crocodile*. Seabury, 1969.
_____. *Androcles and the Lion*. McGraw-Hill, 1970.
_____. *The Town Mouse and the Country Mouse*. McGraw Hill, 1971.
Ginsburg, Mira (Ad.). *Three Rolls and One Doughnut: Fables From Russia*. Il. by Anita
    Lobel. Dial, 1970.
Jacobs, Joseph. *The Fables of Aesop*. Il. by Kurt Wiese. Macmillan, 1980.
Kent, Jack. *More Fables of Aesop*. Parent's, 1974.
McGovern, Ann. *Hee Haw*. Il. by Eric von Schmidt. Houghton, 1969.
Plante, Patricia and David Bergman. *The Turtle and the Two Ducks*. Il. by Ann Rockwell.
    Crowell, 1981.
Reeves, James. *Fables from Aesop*. Il. by Maurice Wilson. Walck, 1962.
Rice, Eve (Adap. and Il.). *Once In a Wood: Ten Tales From Aesop*. Greenwillow,
    1979.

Showalter, Jean B. *The Donkey Ride*. Il. by Tomi Ungerer. Doubleday, 1967.

Stevens, Bryna (Ed.). *Borrowed Feathers and Other Fables*. Il. by Friere Wright and Michael Foreman. Random, 1977.

Untermeyer, Louis. *Aesop's Fables*. Il. by Alice and Martin Provensen. Golden, 1966.

Weil, Lisl. *When Animals Had Fire*. Atheneum, 1982.

Wildsmith, Brian (Il.). *The Lion and the Rat*. Watts, 1963.

_____. *The North Wind and the Sun*. Watts, 1963.

_____. *The Rich Man and the Shoemaker*. Watts, 1965.

_____. *The Miller, the Boy, and the Donkey*. Watts, 1969.

Young, Ed (Il.). *The Lion and the Mouse*. Doubleday, 1979.

Pourquoi Stories

Pourquoi or "why" stories explain animal traits and characteristics or customs of people. Conceptually, these stories may be too difficult for most primary grade children. Therefore, numerous activities involving pourquoi stories are inappropriate. These stories, however, do make enjoyable read-alouds for children.

Some suggested high-ability Pourquoi Story titles follow:

Aardema, Verma (Ret.). *Why Mosquitoes Buzz in People's Ears*. Il. by Leo and Diane Dillon. Dial, 1975.

_____. *Half-a-Ball-of-Kenki*. Il. by Diana Stanley Zuromskis. Warne, 1979.

Baylor, Byrd (Coll.). *And It is Still That Way*. Scribner's, 1976.

Belting, Natalia. *The Long-Tailed Bear and Other Indian Legends*. Il. by Louis Cary. Bobbs-Merrill, 1961.

Bernstein, Margery and Janet Kobrin. *The First Morning*. Scribner's, 1976.

_____. *Coyote Goes Hunting For Fire*. Scribner's, 1974.

_____. *How the Sun Made a Promise and Kept It*. Scribner's, 1974.

Bowden, Joan Chase. *Why the Tides Ebb and Flow*. Il. by Marc Brown. Houghton, 1979.

Cleaver, Nancy. *How the Chipmunk Got Its Stripes*. Scholastic.

Dayrell, Elphinstone. *Why the Sun and the Moon Live In the Sky*. Il. by Blair Lent. Houghton, 1968.

de Paolo, Tomie (Adapt.). *The Prince of the Dolomites*. Harcourt, 1980.

Elkin, Benjamin. *Why the Sun Was Late*. Il. by Jerome Snyder. Parent's, 1966.

Gerson, Mary-Joan (Ret.). *Why the Sky is Far Away*. Il. by Hope Merryman. Harcourt, 1974.

Ginsburg, Mirra. *How the Sun Was Brought Back to the Sky*. Il. by Jose Aruego and Arian Dewey. Macmillan, 1975.

Hodges, Margaret (Ret.). *The Fire Bringer*. Il. by Peter Parnall. Little, Brown, 1972.

Janosch. *Joshua and the Magic Fiddle*. World, 1967.

Kipling, Rudyard. *How the Leopard Got His Spots*. Il. by Leonard Weisgard. Walker & Co., 1972.

_____. *How the Rhinoceros Got His Skin*. Il. by Leonard Weisgard. Walker & Co., 1973.

Leach, Maria. *How the People Sang the Mountains Up*. By Glen Rounds. Viking, 1967.

Luzzatto, Paolo Caboara. *Long Ago When the Earth Was Flat; Three Tales From Africa*. Il. by Aimone Sambuy. Collins, 1980.

McKee, David. *The Day the Tide Went Out... And Out... And Out... And Out... And Out... And Out*. Abelard-Schuman, 1975.

Robbins, Ruth (Ret. and Il.). *How the First Rainbow Was Made: An American Indian Tale*. Parnassus/Houghton, 1980.

Rockwell, Ann. *The Dancing Stars, An Iroquois Legend*. Crowell, 1972.

Rose, Anne K. (Adapt.). *Spider in the Sky*. By Gail Owens. Harper & Row, 1978.

Toye, William. *The Loon's Necklace*. Il. by Elizabeth Cleaver. Oxford, 1977.

_____. *The Fire Stealer*. Il. by Elizabeth Cleaver. Oxford, 1980.

Wicker, Irene. *How the Ocelots Got Their Spots*. Il. by Catherine Perrot. Lyle Stuart, 1976.

Activities for high ability children:

1) Critical reading skills may be enhanced by having children compare different versions of the same pourquoi tale. For example, there are many differences between Kipling's *How the Leopard Got His Spots* and *Half-a-Ball-of-Kenki*, Aardema's tale of why leopards have spots.

2) After the children have heard several "why" stories, they may write some short pourquoi tales of their own.

3) Fact vs. fiction games such as *Why the Sun and the Moon Live in the Sky* activity described on the following page may be developed. Different pourquoi stories may serve as the theme of the game.

Use this as the model for a large game board.

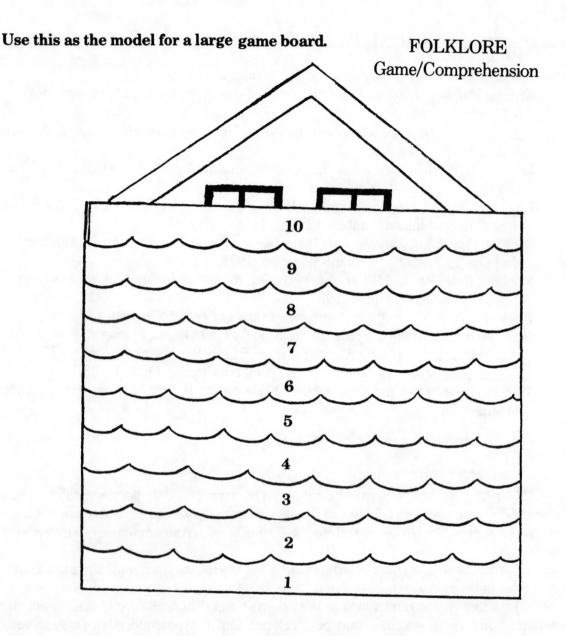

"Why the Sun and the Moon Live in the Sky" is a game involving the comprehension skill of distinguishing fact and fiction. The game board can be made from posterboard. A pocket envelope should be attached to the back of the game board to hold game cards, a set of directions for playing, and an answer key card for checking in case of questions during play. Game pieces are a sun and a moon, also made from posterboard. Game cards should be of two kinds: fact and fiction cards and WET FEET cards. All cards should be mixed to form one deck, so that WET FEET cards are randomly distributed through the deck. Two players may play. Each player selects a game piece, either the sun or the moon. Players roll a die to determine who begins the game. First player draws a card, reads the statement, and identifies it as "fact" or "fiction." When a player gives a correct answer, he/she may move ahead one water level. If a player happens to draw a WET FEET card, he/she must move back one. The first player to reach the top wins the game.

SAMPLE CARDS

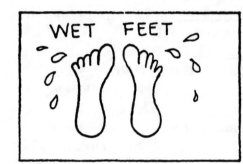

GAME PIECES

Suggestions for fact and fiction cards:

FACT:

— The sun is our nearest star.
— Our planet Earth revolves around the sun.
— Some planets have more than one moon.
— The moon is closer to the Earth than the sun is.
— The moon has large craters.
— We would not weigh very much on the moon.
— The moon is smaller than the sun.

FICTION:

— The moon is a star.
— The moon is made of green cheese.
— Earth has two moons.
— People could live on the sun.
— The moon shines only at night.
— No one has ever walked on the moon.
— The sun does not shine on cloudy days.
— There is a man in the moon.

45

SELECTED BIBLIOGRAPHY OF FOLK TALES

Aardema, Verna. *Who's In Rabbit's House?* Il. by Leo and Diane Dillon. Dial, 1977. (Africa).

_____. *The Riddle of the Drum: A Tale From Tizapan, Mexico.* Il. by Tony Chen. Four Winds, 1979. (Mexico).

_____. *Bringing the Rain to Kapiti Plain.* Il. by Beatriz Vidal. Dial, 1981.

Anderson, Hans Christian. *The Emperor's New Clothes.* Il. by Virginia Burton. Houghton, 1949.

_____. *The Emperor's New Clothes.* Il. by Jack and Irene Delane. Random, 1971.

_____. *The Nightingale.* Trans. by Eva Le Gallienne. Il. by Nancy Ekholm Burkert. Harper & Row, 1965.

_____. *The Ugly Duckling.* Il. by Adrienne Adams. Scribner, 1965.

_____. *The Ugly Duckling.* Retold and Il. by Lorinda Bryan Cauley. Harcourt, 1979.

_____. *The Fir Tree.* Il. by Nancy Ekholm Burkert. Harper & Row, 1970.

_____. *The Princess and the Pea.* Il. by Paul Galdone. Seabury, 1978.

_____. *The Princess and the Pea.* Il. by Janet Stevens. Holiday, 1982.

_____. *Thumbelina.* Il. by Adrienne Adams. Scribner, 1961.

_____. *Thumbelina.* Adapted by Amy Ehrlich. Il. by Susan Jeffers. Dial, 1979.

_____. *Thumbelina.* Trans. by Richard and Clara Winston. Il. by Lisbeth Zwerger. Morrow, 1980.

Aruego, Jose and Ariane Aruego. *A Crocodile's Tale.* Scribner's, 1972. (Philippines).

Asbjornsen, Peter Christian and Jorgen E. Moe. *The Three Billy Goats Gruff.* Il. by Marcia Brown. Harcourt, 1957.

Baker, Betty. *And Me, Coyote!* Il. by Maria Horvath. Macmillan, 1982. (Native American).

Basile, Giambattista. *Petrosinella.* Il. by Diane Stanley. Warne, 1981. (Neapolitan Rapunzel).

Bell, Anthea. *The Swineherd.* Il. by Lisbeth Zwerger. Greenwillow, 1982.

Berson, Harold (Adapt.). *Charles and Claudine.* Macmillan, 1980 (France).

Blevgad, Erik (Il.). *The Three Little Pigs.* Atheneum, 1980.

Brown, Marcia. *Stone Soup.* Scribner, 1947.

_____. *The Blue Jackal.* Scribner, 1977.

Bryan, Ashley. *The Ox of the Wonderful Horns and Other African Folktales.* Atheneum, 1971. (Africa).

Bryant, Sara Cone. *The Burning Rice Fields.* Il. by Mamoru Funai. Holt, 1963. (Japan).

Carle, Eric. *Eric Carle's Storybook.* Watts, 1976.

Cauley, Lorinda Bryan (Adapt. and Il.). *The Goose and the Golden Coins.* Harcourt, 1981.

_____. *The Cock, the Mouse and the Little Red Hen*. Putnam, 1982.

Coombs, Patricia. *The Magic Pot*. Lothrop, 1977.

Cooney, Barbara (Ret. and Il.). *Little Brother and Little Sister*. Doubleday, 1982.

Cooper, Susan (Adapt.). *The Silver Cow: A Welsh Tale*. Il. by Warwick Hutton. Atheneum, 1983.

Daniels, Guy (Trans.). *Foma the Terrible*. Il. by Imero Gobbato. Delacorte, 1970. (Russia).

De Beaumont, Maria Leprince. *Beauty and the Beast*. Trans by Richard Howard. Il. by Hilary Knight. Macmillan, 1963.

De La Mare, Walter. *Molly Whuppie*. Il. by Errol Le Cain. Farrar, Straus and Giroux, 1983.

de Paola, Tomie. *Strega Nona*. Prentice-Hall, 1975. (Italy).

_____. *The Clown of God*. Harcourt, 1978. (Italy).

_____. *The Lady of Guadalupe*. Holiday, 1980. (Mexico).

de Regniers, Beatrice Schenk. *Red Riding Hood*. Il. by Edward Gorey. Atheneum, 1972.

_____. (Ad.). *Everyone is Good for Something*. Il. by Margot Tomes. Houghton, 1980.

Dewey, Ariane. *The Thunder God's Sun*. Greenwillow, 1981. (Peru).

Domanska, Janina. *Little Red Hen*. Macmillan, 1973.

_____. *The Turnip*. Macmillan, 1969. (Russia).

_____. (Adapt. and Il.). *A Scythe, a Rooster, and a Cat*. Greenwillow, 1981. (Russia).

Duff, Maggie. *The Princess and the Pumpkin*. Il. by Catherine Stock. Macmillan, 1980. (Majorca).

Ehrlich, May (Ret.). *The Wild Swans*. Il. by Susan Jeffers. Dial, 1981.

_____. *The Snow Queen*. Il. by Susan Jeffers. Dial, 1982.

Fritz, Jean. *The Good Giants and the Bad Pukwudgies*. Il by Tomie de Paola. Putnam, 1982. (Native American).

Gackenbach, Dick. *Arabella and Mr. Crack*. Macmillan, 1982.

Galdone, Paul. *The Three Wishes*. McGraw-Hill, 1961.

_____. *The Three Little Pigs*. Seabury, 1970.

_____. *The Three Bears*. Seabury, 1972.

_____. *The Three Billy Goats Gruff*. Seabury, 1973.

_____. *The Table, the Donkey and the Stick*. McGraw-Hill, 1976.

_____. *What's in Fox's Sack?* Houghton/Clarion, 1982.

Goble, Paul. *The Girl Who Loved Wild Horses*. Bradbury, 1978. (Native American).

_____. *The Gift of the Sacred Dog*. Bradbury, 1980. (Native American).

_____. *Star Boy*. Bradbury, 1983. (Native American).

Goode, Diane (Il.). *Beauty and the Beast*. Bradbury, 1978.

Grimm. *Little Red Riding Hood*. Il. by Trina Schart Hyman. Holiday, 1983.

_____. *The Devil with the Three Golden Hairs*. Adapted and Il. by Nonny Hogrogian. Knopf, 1983.

_____. *Rapunzel*. Il. by Felix Hoffman. Harcourt, 1961.

_____. *Rapunzel*. Retold and Il. by Jutta Ash. Holt, 1982.

_____. *Rapunzel*. Retold by Barbara Rogasky. Il. by Trina Schart Hyman. Holiday, 1982.

_____. *Snow White and Rose Red*. Trans. by Wayne Andrew. Il. by Adrienne Adams. Scribner, 1964.

_____. *The Twelve Dancing Princesses*. Trans. by Elizabeth Shub. Il. by Uri Shulevitz. Scribner, 1966.

_____. *Jorinda and Joringel*. Trans. by Elizabeth Shub. Il. by Adrienne Adams. Scribner, 1968.

_____. *Snow White and The Seven Dwarfs*. Trans. by Randall Jarrell. Il. by Nancy Ekholm Burkert. Farrar, 1972.

_____. *Snow White and the Seven Dwarfs*. Retold by Freya Littledale. Il. by Susan Jeffers. Four Winds, 1981.

_____. *Snow White*. Trans. by Paul Heins. Il. by Trina Schart Hyman. Little, Brown, 1974.

_____. *Tom Thumb*. Il. by Felix Hoffmann. Atheneum, 1973.

_____. *Little Red Cap*. Trans. by Elizabeth Crawford. Il. by Lisbeth Zwerger. Morrow, 1983.

_____. *The Frog Prince*. Retold by Edith Tarcov. Il. by James Marshall. Four Winds, 1974.

_____. *The Frog Prince*. Il. by Paul Galdone. McGraw-Hill, 1975.

_____. *The Shoemaker and the Elves*. Retold by Freya Littledale. Il. by Brinton Turkle. Four Winds, 1975.

_____. *The Donkey Prince*. Adapted by M. Jean Craig. Il. by Barbara Cooney. Doubleday, 1977.

_____. *The Twelve Dancing Princesses*. Il. by Errol Le Cain. Viking, 1978.

_____. *The Seven Ravens*. Retold and Il. by Donna Diamond. Viking, 1979.

_____. *The Bear and the Kingbird*. Trans. by Lore Segal. Il. by Chris Conover. Farrar, 1979.

_____. *The Fisherman and His Wife*. Trans. by Randall Jarrell. Il. by Margot Zemach. Farrar, 1980.

_____. *The Bremen Town Musicians*. Trans. by Elizabeth Shub. Il. by Janina Domanska. Greenwillow, 1980.

_____. *The Bremen Town Musicians*. Retold and Il. by Donna Diamond. Delacorte, 1981.

_____. *The Bremen Town Musicians*. Retold and Il. by Ilse Plume. Doubleday, 1980.

_____. *The Month-Brothers*. Retold by Samuel Marshak. Il. by Diane Stanley. Morrow, 1983 (Czech).

Hague, Kathleen and Michael (Ret.). *East of the Sun and West of the Moon*. Il. by Michael Hague. Harcourt, 1980.

Haley, Gail. *A Story A Story*. Atheneum, 1970 (Africa).

Hamilton, Virginia. *Jahdu*. Il. by Jerry Pinkney. Greenwillow, 1980.

Hirsch, Marilyn. *Could Anything Be Worse?* Holiday, 1974.

Hodges, Margaret. *The Wave*. Il. by Blair Lent. Houghton, 1964 (Japan).

Hogrogian, Nonny. *One Fine Day*. Macmillan, 1971.

Houston, James. *Kiviok's Magic Journey*. Atheneum, 1973 (Eskimo).

Hunter, Mollie. *A Furl of Fairy Wind*. Il. by Stephen Gammell. Harper, 1977.

Jacobs, Joseph. *King of the Cats*. Adapt. and Il. by Paul Galdone. Houghton, 1980.

_____. *Three Little Pigs*. Il. by Lorinda Bryan Cauley. Putnam, 1980.

_____. *The Three Sillies*. Adapt. and Il. by Paul Galdone. Houghton/Clarion, 1981.

Jaquith, Priscilla. *Bo Rabbit Smart for True: Folktales from the Gullah*. Il. by Ed Young. Philomel, 1981.

Jeffers, Susan. *Wild Robin*. Dutton, 1976.

Kent, Jack. *The Fat Cat*. Parent's, 1971.

Lifton, Betty Jean. *The Mud Snail Son*. Il. by Fuku Akino. Atheneum, 1971. (Japan).

Lobel, Arnold. *Ming Lo Moves the Mountain*. Greenwillow, 1982. (China).

Matsutani, Miyoko. *The Crane Maiden*. Il. by Chihiro Iwasaki. Parent's, 1968. (Japan).

Mayer, Marianna (Adapt.). *Beauty and the Beast*. Il by Mercer Mayer. Four Winds, 1978.

_____. *East of the Sun and West of the Moon*. Il. by Mercer Mayer. Four Winds, 1980.

Mayer, Mercer (Il.). *Favorite Tales From Grimm*. Four Winds, 1982.

McDermott, Beverly Brodsky (Adapt. and Il.). *The Crystal Apple*. Viking, 1974. (Russia).

McDermott, Gerald. *Anansi the Spider*. Holt, 1972. (Africa).

_____. *Arrow to the Sun*. Viking, 1974. (Native American).

Mosel, Arlene. *Tikki Tikki Tembo*. Il. by Blair Lent. Holt, 1968. (China).

_____. *The Funny Little Woman*. Il. by Blair Lent. Dutton, 1972. (Japan).

Pearce, Philippa. *Beauty and the Beast*. Il. by Alan Barnett. Crowell, 1972.

Peppe, Rodney (Ret. and Il.). *Three Little Pigs*. Lothrop, 1979.

Perrault, Charles. *The Little Red Riding Hood*. Il. by William Stobbs. Walck, 1972.

Pincus, Harriet (Il.). *Little Red Riding Hood*. Harcourt, 1968.

Ransome, Arthur. *The Fool of the World and the Flying Ship*. Il. by Uri Shulevits. Farrar, 1968. (Russia).

Riordan, James and Eileen Colwell. *Little Gray Neck*. Il. by Caroline Sharpe. Addison-Wesley, 1976. (Russia).

Rockwell, Anne. *The Three Bears and 15 Other Stories*. Crowell, 1975.

_____. *The Old Woman and Her Pig and Ten Other Stories*. Crowell, 1979.

San Souci, Robert (Adapt.). *The Brave Little Tailor*. Il. by Daniel San Souci. Doubleday, 1982.

Shub, Elizabeth (Adapt.). *Clever Kate*. Il. by Anita Lobel. Macmillan, 1973.

Shulevitz, Uri. *The Treasure*. Farrar, 1979.

Sleator, William. *The Angry Moon*. Il. by Blair Lent. Little, Brown, 1981.

Small, Ernest. *Baba Yaga*. Il. by Blair Lent. Houghton, 1966. (Russia).

Tate, Joan (Trans). *The Runaway Pancake*. Il. by Svend Otto. Larousse, 1980.

Titiev, Estelle and Lila Pargment (Trans.). *How the Moolah Was Taught a Lesson and*

Other Tales from Russia. Il. by Ray Cruz. Dial, 1976.

Towle, Faith. *The Magic Cooking Pot*. Houghton, 1975.

Tresselt, Alvin and Nancy Cleaver. *The Legend of the Willow Plate*. Il. by Joseph Low. Parent's, 1968.

Van Woerkom, Dorothy (Adapt.). *The Friends of Abu Ali; Three More Tales of The Middle East*. Il. by Harold Berson. Macmillan, 1978.

Werth, Kurt (Ret. and Il.). *Lazy Jack*. Viking, 1970.

Wilde, Oscar. *The Selfish Giant*. Il. by Michael Foreman and Freire Wright. Methuen, 1978.

Williams, Jay. *Seven at One Blow*. Il. by Friso Henstra. Parent's, 1972.

Yolen, Jane. *The Emperor and the Kite*. Il. by Ed Young. World, 1967. (China).

_____. *The Girl Who Cried Flowers and Other Tales*. Il by David Palladini. Crowell, 1974.

Zemach, Harve (Adapt.). *Nail Soup*. Il by Margot Zemach. Follett, 1964.

Zemach, Margot. *The Three Sillies*. Holt, 1963.

_____. *It Could Always Be Worse*. Farrar, 1977.

CHAPTER FOUR

Fantasy

Fantasy
Involving Human Characters

This center is composed of three stations: 1) A reading skills station based on *The Sweet Touch* by Lorna Balian; 2) a creative writing station based on David McPhail's *The Cereal Box*; and 3) a vocabulary station based on *The Remarkable Plant in Apartment 4* by Guilio Maestro. These books should be read to the children prior to introducing the center activities.

HUMAN FANTASY   Skills Station/*The Sweet Touch*

Independent Activities:

1) **"31 Flavors"** — Alphabetical Order Ice Cream Cones. Children alphabetize ice cream flavors by arranging individual "dips" of ice cream on a cone. Cones and dips of ice cream should be made from laminated construction paper or poster board. Ice cream flavors should be in different colors. The difficulty of the alphabetizing (first letter, second letter, etc.) and the number of flavor names to be alphabetized should be determined by the ability levels of the children. See illustration on next page. Suggested flavors to alphabetize:

chocolate marshmallow	pineapple	butter pecan
coconut	pistachio	blueberry
chocolate chip	maple nut	caramel twirl
cherry	bubble gum	orange sherbert
chocolate	pralines and cream	butterscotch twirl
peppermint	tutti fruiti	vanilla
peach	butter brickle	strawberry
lemon	mint chocolate chip	raspberry ripple
fudge ripple	black walnut	rocky road
lime sherbert	almond crunch	boysenberry
banana		

Each cone and its flavors should be placed in separate envelopes. Dips should be numbered on the back for self-checking.

2) **Compound Cupcakes** — Children are to put two parts of a compound word together by placing the frosting on the cupcake. This activity can be made self-checking by varying the way the two pieces fit together, like a puzzle. Cupcakes should be made from laminated poster board. **See illustration on page 55.**

3) **Contraction Cookie Jar** — In this activity, children match two words with their contracted form. Cover a large coffee can with colorful contact paper and label it "Cookies." The "cookies" should be made from laminated construction paper cut into a variety of familiar cookie shapes. Cookies should have either the two words or the contraction written on them. Each cookie should have a mate. Children are to dump out the cookies and match the pairs. Shape of the cookie should *not* be a factor in the matching. The emphasis is on matching the words with the correct contraction. For self-checking, cookies should be coded on the back. See illustration on next page.

4) **Lifesaver Rhyming Words** — Children make a "roll" of lifesavers by placing all the rhyming words together. Lifesavers should be made from assorted colors of laminated construction paper cut approximately 3½" in diameter. Cover and decorate an oatmeal box to resemble a roll of lifesavers and keep the pieces in it. All the lifesavers that have words from the same rhyming family should be coded in the same way on the back for self-checking. Several word families should be included and can be changed often.

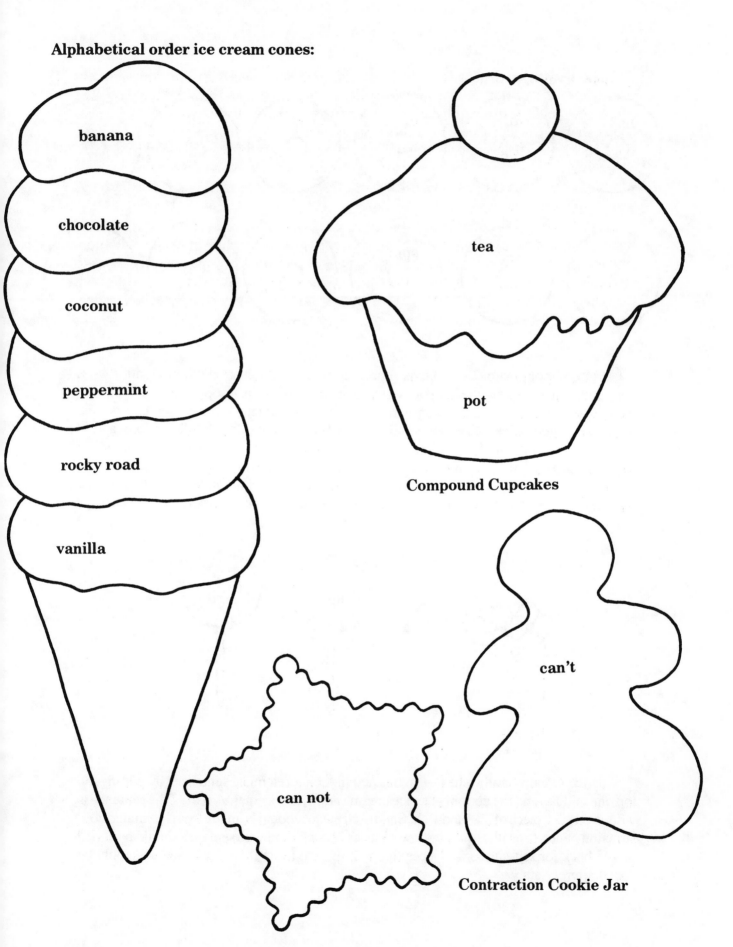

Alphabetical order ice cream cones:

banana

chocolate

coconut

peppermint

rocky road

vanilla

tea

pot

Compound Cupcakes

can not

can't

Contraction Cookie Jar

55

Lifesaver rhyming words

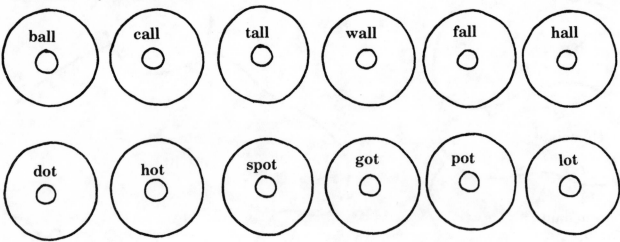

5) **"Lollipopposites"** — This is a partner activity in which children identify word opposites. On one side of the lollipop is a word; on the other side, its opposite. Lollipops are made from laminated construction paper (cut 2½" in diameter) in assorted colors, and wooden ice cream sticks. The stick should be glued *between* two paper circles to form a front and back of the lollipop. Keep lollipops in a small coffee can covered with colorful contact paper. To do this activity, a child picks a lollipop from the can and shows his/her partner one side of it. The partner names a word opposite. Play proceeds through all the lollipops. The partners then exchange lollipops and go through them again. Partners self-check each other.

6) **Ice Cream Sandwiches** — In this activity, children make sentences by putting the top, the middle, and the bottom of an ice cream sandwich together. A part of the sentence is written on each piece of the sandwich. Sandwich pieces should be made from laminated construction paper. (See illustration below.) Pieces of each sandwich sentence should be coded on the back for self-checking. Pieces that will fit with more than one sentence should be coded appropriately.

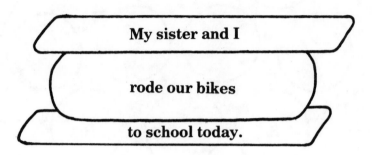

My sister and I

rode our bikes

to school today.

7) **Gum Ball Rally** — This activity reinforces phonics sounds. Initial and final consonant sounds, long and short vowel sounds, or consonant blends and digraphs may be used. A large outline of a gum ball machine that can be spread on the floor is needed. The gumball machine could be made from the paper used for bulletin board backgrounds that comes on large rolls, plain wrapping paper on a roll, or a thin sheet of plastic. Colorful "gum balls," each with a sound written on it, are scattered on the gum ball machine. Children may play individually, with partners, or on teams. A player flips a penny so that it lands on a gum ball. He/she must then give a word that contains the sound written on that gum ball. Other players act as "judge." Gum balls should not be permanently attached so that the activity can be changed as often as desired.

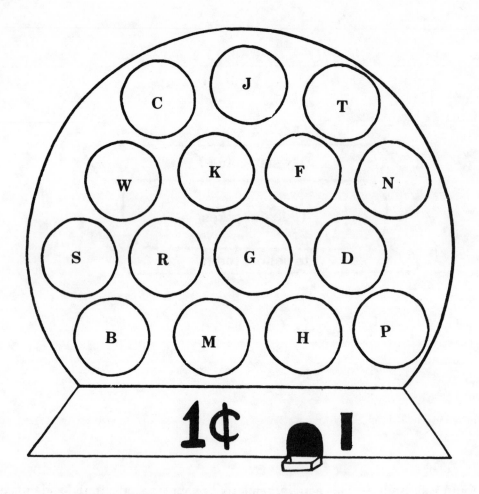

Other Activities:

1) **Design a candy bar.** Have each student invent a new kind of candy bar. Children will need to decide on a name for the candy bar, draw what the wrapper will look like, and list the ingredients (chocolate, peanuts, marshmallow, caramel, etc.). Higher ability students might carry the activity further and develop an advertising campaign for selling their candy bars.

2) **"Sweets" Cookbooks.** Have each child write a recipe for a favorite "sweet." Remind them that they must include the ingredients, directions for preparing, and the time and temperature for cooking (if appropriate). Duplicate their recipes and bind them together so that each child may have a copy of the "cookbook" to take home. (Mother or Dad probably won't want to try any of these recipes, but they will certainly enjoy reading them!)

3) **Making "Sweets."** The recipes suggested below do not require baking or cooking on the stove.

PEANUT BUTTER CREAMS·

1   egg
⅓   cup peanut butter
1   T. soft margarine
½   t. vanilla
2   cups powdered sugar
     salted peanuts, finely chopped

Beat egg. Beat in peanut butter, margarine, vanilla and 1 cup powdered sugar. Then, stir in 1 more cup powdered sugar. Shape dough into tiny balls. Roll each ball in finely chopped, salted peanuts. Place on waxed paper and refrigerate until firm.
Makes about 36 candies.

NO-BAKE COOKIES·

1   (12 oz.) box vanilla wafers
1½ cups powdered sugar
1½ cups coconut
½   cup chopped nuts
1   (16 oz.) can frozen orange juice, thawed

Crush the vanilla wafers. Mix all ingredients well. Shape into small balls and roll in powdered sugar.

NO-BAKE COOKIES·

1 package graham crackers, crushed
1 jar marshmallow creme

Roll together. Top with the following: nuts, chocolate chips, coconut, maraschino cherries

HUMAN FANTASY   Creative Writing Station/"The Cereal Box"

No special arrangement is needed for this station. All activities may be placed on a table. Have the children bring in empty cereal boxes for the set-up of this center. The boxes will serve as containers for the books and activities. In each cereal box, place a book and an index card containing a creative writing idea based on that book. Many children will be able to read the books themselves. If the skills of the children are not sufficient to do so, however, the teacher may want to record some of the books on cassette tape. The tape can then be placed in the cereal box along with the book and idea card, and the children can listen to the story. Some of the children may wish to share some of their efforts and leave their stories in the boxes for others to read. These activities present a good opportunity to stress proofreading and the importance of writing in good form for others to read.

Suggested below are some books and creative writing ideas. The teacher will want to add his/her own ideas to this list. In some cases, an art activity is suggested to accompany the creative writing. All references can be found in the bibliography at the end of this section.

Gia and the One Hundred Dollars Worth of Bubble Gum (Frank Asch)
  1. If someone gave you a hundred dollars, how would you spend it? Write a story.
  2. Write a story about your adventures that starts like this:
     One day I blew a bubble *so* big that. . .

Cloudy with a Chance of Meatballs (Judith Barrett)
  1. Write a weather forecast for the town of Chewandswallow.
  2. What if it rained chocolate? Write a story.

Come Away from the Water, Shirley (John Burningham)

Time to Get Out of the Bath, Shirley (John Burningham)
  Write another adventure for Shirley.

Would You Rather . . . (John Burningham)
  Choose any page in the book and write a story about what you would rather do and tell why you chose that.

Barney Bipple's Magic Dandelions (Carol Chapman)
  If you had a magic dandelion, what would you wish for? Write a story.

The Gorilla Did It (Barbara S. Hazen)

The Bear's Toothache (David McPhail)
  Choose a very big animal that you would like to have come into your room. Write a story about what you would do together. Tell about some problems you might have.

Can I Keep Him? (Steven Kellogg)

If you could have any animal you wanted for a pet, what would you pick? Write a story about this pet.

Bubble Bubble (Mercer Mayer)

This book has no words. Write a story to go with the pictures.

A Special Trick (Mercer Mayer)

If you could do a magic trick, what would you do? Write a story about your trick and be sure to put in your magic words.

Pickle Creature (D. Manus Pinkwater)

Write a story about another kind of vegetable creature. Draw a picture of your creature to go with your story.

The Big Orange Splot (D. Manus Pinkwater)

If you could have a house that looked like anything you wanted, what would it be? Write a story about your house and draw a picture of it.

The Cereal Box (David McPhail)

Invent a new cereal. What is its name? What does it taste like? What does it look like? What kind of surprises can you find in the box? What will you tell people about your cereal so that they will want to buy it? Draw a picture of the front of your cereal box.

What Are We Going to Do About Andrew (Marjorie W. Sharmat)

1. If you could fly, write a story about where you would go.
2. If you could turn into an animal, what would you turn into? Write a story about yourself as an animal.

Bored — Nothing to Do! (Peter Spier)

1. Write a story about something that you made or built.
2. If you could build something, what would you build? Write a story about how you would build it.

Applebaum's Have a Robot (Jane Thayer)

The Robot Birthday (Eve Bunting)

If you had a robot, what would you have it do for you? What would you name it? What does your robot look like? Draw a picture of your robot to go with your story.

No More Baths (Brock Cole)

Write a story about what *you* do to keep from having to take a bath.

You're a Little Kid With a Big Heart (Bernard Waber)

Write a story about some things you could do if you were grown up that you cannot do now.

The Remarkable Plant in Apartment 4 (Giulio Maestro)

1. If you had a remarkable plant like this one, what would you use it for?
2. Write a newspaper headline about what happened in the story. Write a newspaper story telling only the *most important* things that happened in the book.

1) **Context Clues** — In this activity children will use context to supply the missing word in a sentence. Make flower pots and write on each one a sentence, leaving out one word. The children are to slip a flower containing the missing word into the correct flower pot. Flowers and pots should be made from laminated construction paper or poster board. See illustration below. Code the flowers and pots for self-checking.

2) **"Nyms" Match** — For this activity, you will need three clay flower pots and some flowers made from laminated construction paper or poster board. (See drawings below.) Label the pots as follows:

> homonyms — two words that sound the same but have different meanings.
> synonyms — two words that have almost the same meaning.
> antonyms — two words that are opposites.

There should be two sets of flowers, in two different colors, in each pot. On one set of flowers, write a series of words. On the second set of flowers, write each word's homonym/synonym/ antonym. Children are to put the contents of a pot on the table and match the pairs. Code matching pairs on the back for self-checking. Children should do each pot individually.

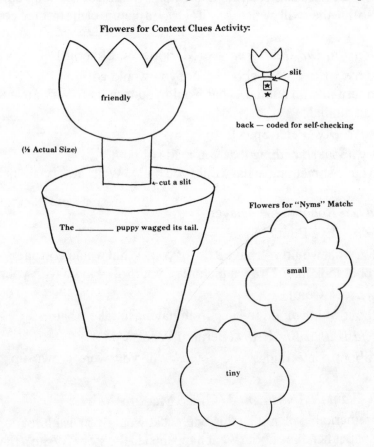

Flowers for Context Clues Activity:

friendly

slit

back — coded for self-checking

(¼ Actual Size)

←cut a slit

The _____ puppy wagged its tail.

Flowers for "Nyms" Match:

small

tiny

3) **Sight Words Check** — For this activity you will need a tall area for displaying a sunflower-like plant. This plant can be made from construction paper. Each child does this activity individually with the teacher, aide, or other adult. It involves checking the children on their recognition of basic sight words or vocabulary words taken from their reading books.

You will need to prepare a set of word cards at three different difficulty levels for each of your reading groups. For example, for children reading at the first reader level, you would need a set of preprimer words, primer words, and first reader level words. (The most difficult set of words should correspond to the instructional reading level of the children.)

Each child has a petal that has his/her name on it. All the petals are placed at ground level to start. Once a child has mastered the easiest set of word cards, he/she moves the petal to the lowest level of leaves. The child moves up to the next level on the plant after mastering the second set of cards. After the child successfully pronounces the last set of words, he/she places his/her petal on the flower. The objective is to fill the flower with petals containing the names of all the children.

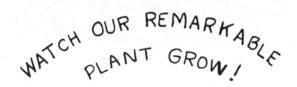

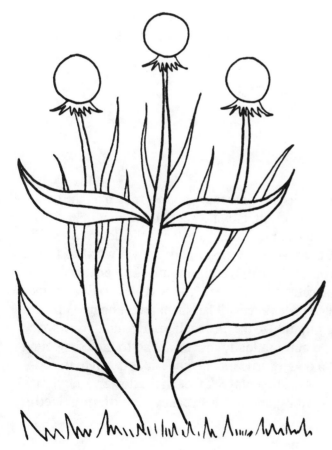

4) **Worksheet** — The worksheet is based on the book *The Remarkable Plant in Apartment 4*. The book should be available for the children to use if needed.

5) **"Monster Vine"** — Game. This game deals with the identification of homographs. A homograph is a word that has different meanings when used in different contexts. To play this game, you will need to make the game board shown on the next page and a set of playing cards. Each card contains two definitions of a homograph. There should also be a number — 1, 2, or 3 — in the lower right corner of each card to indicate the number of spaces on the gameboard that a player can move.

Listed on the next page are some suggested playing cards:

It flies at night.
You hit a ball with it.
(bat)

A place to keep money.
The edge of a river.
(bank)

A noise a dog makes.
The covering for a tree.
(bark)

You wear it on your finger.
A noise made by a bell.
(ring)

You use it to tell time.
When you look at something.
(watch)

A place to put clothes.
The front of your body.
(chest)

Something you put on a letter.
When you bang the floor with your feet.
(stamp)

Go over and over down a hill.
A kind of bread.
(roll)

Something written on a calendar.
A brown dried fruit.
(date)

A spinning toy.
The opposite of *bottom*.
(top)

A stone.
Move back and forth.
(rock)

You write with it.
A pig can live in it.
(pen)

A toy you can bounce and roll.
The dance Cinderella went to.
(ball)

You hit it with a hammer.
It grows at the end of your finger.
(nail)

What you do after school.
Actors put on this on a stage.
(play)

CARD

The teacher will want to add others to this list. Two to four children may play the game. Playing pieces may be cardboard, plastic, cloth, etc., flowers in different colors. The playing cards are placed face down on the game board. A roll of a die determines who begins the game. A player draws a card, reads it aloud and gives a word to fit the definitions. If the word is correct, the player then moves the number of spaces indicated on the card. If the player answers incorrectly, play moves to the next player. Each player must perform the action written in the space on which he/she lands. The two upward leaves and three downward vines add variation to the moves. If a player lands on a space with one of the upward leaves, he/she automatically moves ahead to the connecting space. Likewise, if a player lands on a downward vine, he/she slides down to the connecting space. The winner of the game is the first player to reach the flower. Encourage the children to play until all have finished the game. An answer key should be provided in case of disagreement.

Read *The Remarkable Plant in Apartment 4*.
Read the sentences and write the answers in the boxes.
Use the words below to help you.
Then take the *first* letter of every word and write it in the spaces at the bottom of the page to find out what kind of plant it was.

eat   buds   Michael   roots   Apartment 4
room   electric   kitchen   admiring   leaves

This part of a plant grows below the ground.

Mr. Rotondo could not _____ his breakfast because of the plant.

The boy in the story is named_____.

Where do the boy and his parents live?

Where did the boy put the plant to grow?

What don't you need when you camp out?

The next day everyone was _____ the plant.

Before a flower opens, it is a _____.

A plant has many green _____.

Michael and his father put _____ trains all over the plant.

What kind of plant is it?

___ ___ ___ ___ ___ ___ ___ ___ ___ ___

65

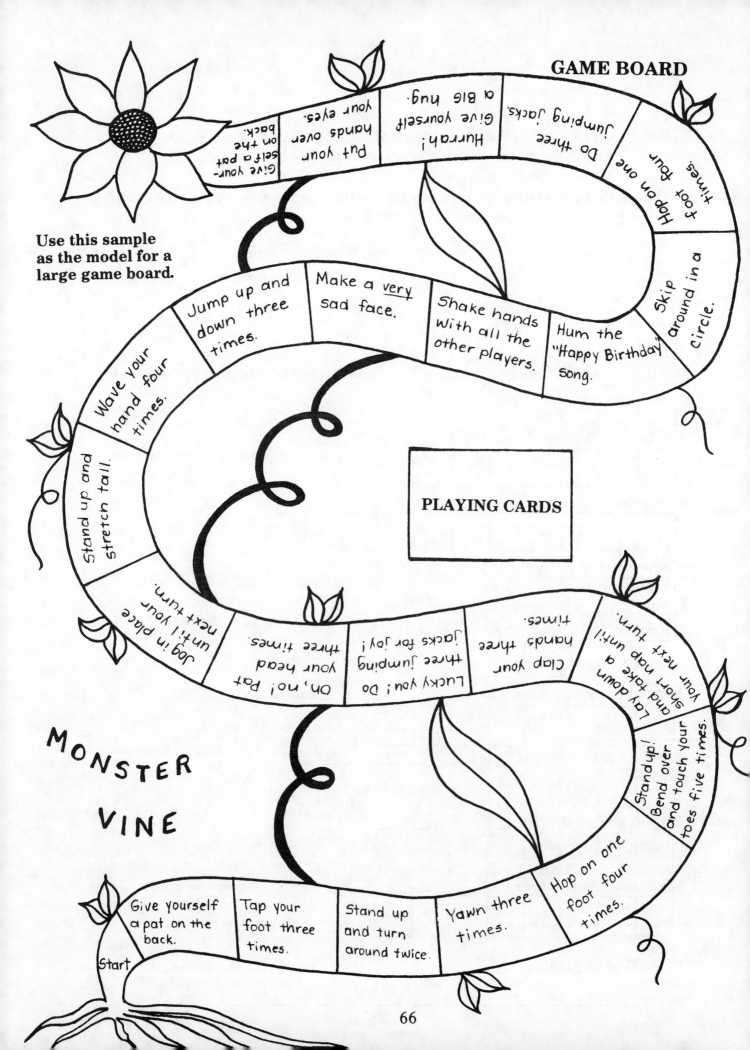

GAME BOARD

Use this sample as the model for a large game board.

Give yourself a pat on the back.

Put your hands over your eyes.

Hurrah! Give yourself a Big hug.

Do three jumping jacks.

Hop on one foot four times.

Skip around in a circle.

Jump up and down three times.

Make a very sad face.

Shake hands with all the other players.

Hum the "Happy Birthday" song.

Wave your hand four times.

Stand up and stretch tall.

PLAYING CARDS

Jog in place until your next turn.

Oh, no! Pat your head three times.

Lucky you! Do three jumping jacks for joy!

Clap your hands three times.

Lay down and take a short nap until your next turn.

Stand up! Bend over and touch your toes five times.

Hop on one foot four times.

MONSTER VINE

Give yourself a pat on the back.

Tap your foot three times.

Stand up and turn around twice.

Yawn three times.

Start

66

SELECTED BIBLIOGRAPHY OF FANTASY BOOKS
INVOLVING HUMAN CHARACTERS

Alexander, Martha. *Marty McGee's Space Lab, No Girls Allowed*. Dial, 1981.

Anno, Mitsumasa. *The King's Flower*. Collins, 1979.

Ardizzone, Edward. *Ship's Cook Ginger*. Macmillan, 1978.

Asch, Frank. *Gia and the One Hundred Dollars Worth of Bubble Gum*. McGraw-Hill, 1974.

Balian, Lorna. *Humbug Witch*. Abingdon, 1965.

_____. *The Sweet Touch*. Abingdon, 1976.

Barrett, Judith. *Cloudy With a Chance of Meatballs*. Il. by Ron Barrett. Atheneum, 1978.

Benjamin, Alan. *A Change of Plans*. Il. by Steven Kellogg. Four Winds, 1982.

Bunting, Eve. *The Robot Birthday*. Il. by Marie De John. Dutton, 1980

Burningham, John. *Come Away From the Water, Shirley*. Crowell, 1977.

_____. *Time to Get Out of the Bath, Shirley*. Crowell, 1977.

_____. *Would You Rather* . . . Crowell, 1978.

Chapman, Carol. *Barney Bipple's Magic Dandelions*. Il. by Steven Kellogg. Dutton, 1977.

Choate, Judith. *Awful Alexander*. Il. by Steven Kellogg. Doubleday, 1976.

Cole, Brock. *No More Baths*. Doubleday, 1980.

Coombs, Patricia. *Lisa and the Grompet*. Lothrop, 1970.

Dillon, Barbara. *The Beast in the Bed*. Il. by Chris Conover. Morrow, 1981.

Edmondson, Madeleine. *Anna Witch*. Il. by William Pene du Bois. Doubleday, 1982.

Flora, James. *The Great Green Turkey Creek Monster*. Atheneum, 1976.

_____. *Wanda and the Bumbly Wizard*. Atheneum, 1980.

Fox, Paula. *Hungry Fred*. Il. by Rosemary Wells. Bradbury, 1969.

Galdone, Joanna. *The Tailypo, a Ghost Story*. Il. by Paul Galdone. Seabury, 1977.

Gibbons, Gail. *The Too-Great Bread Bake Book*. Warne, 1980.

Haas, Irene. *The Maggie B.*. Atheneum, 1975.

Hanlon, Emily *What if a Lion Eats Me and I Fall Into a Hippopotamus' Mud Hole?* Il. by Leigh Grant. Delacorte, 1975.

Hazen, Barbara Shook. *The Gorilla Did It*. Il. by Ray Cruz. Atheneum, 1976.

Hoban, Russell. *The Twenty Elephant Restaurant*. Il. by Emily Arnold McCully. Atheneum, 1978.

Horwitz, Elinor L. *When the Sky is Like Lace*. Il. by Barbara Cooney. Lippincott, 1975.

Jeschke, Susan. *Firerose*. Holt, 1974.

Keats, Ezra Jack. *Regards to the Man In the Moon*. Four Winds, 1981.

Kellogg, Steven. *Can I Keep Him?* Dial, 1972.

_____. *Won't Somebody Play With Me?* Dial, 1972.

Krasilovsky, Phyllis. *The Man Who Entered a Contest*. Il. by Yuri Salzman. Doubleday, 1980.

Krensky, Stephen. *The Lion Upstairs*. Il. by Leigh Grant. Atheneum, 1983.

Kumin, Maxine and Anne Sexton. *The Wizard's Tears*. Il. by Evaline Ness. McGraw-Hill, 1975.

Lord, John Vernon. *The Runaway Roller Skate*. Houghton, 1974.

Low, Joseph. *Don't Drag Your Feet*. Atheneum, 1983.

Maestro, Giulio. *The Remarkable Plant in Apartment 4*. Bradbury, 1973.

Mahy, Margaret. *The Boy Who Was Followed Home*. Il. by Steven Kellogg. Watts, 1975.

Marshall, Edward. *Space Case*. Il. by James Marshall. Dial, 1980.

Mayer, Mercer. *There's a Nightmare in My Closet*. Dial, 1968.

——————. *A Special Trick*. Dial, 1970.

——————. *Me and My Flying Machine*. Parent's, 1971.

——————. *Mrs. Beggs and the Wizard*. Parent's, 1973.

——————. *What Do You Do With a Kangaroo?* Four Winds, 1973.

——————. *Appelard and Liverwurst*. Il. by Steven Kellogg. Four Winds, 1978.

McPhail, David. *The Bear's Toothache*. Little, Brown, 1972.

——————. *The Cereal Box*. Little, Brown, 1974.

——————. *The Train*. Little, Brown, 1977.

——————. *The Magical Drawings of Moony B. Finch*. Doubleday, 1978.

Naylor, Phyllis Reynolds. *The Boy with the Helium Head*. Il. by Kay Chorao. Atheneum, 1982.

Noble, Trinka Hakes. *The Day Jimmy's Boa Ate the Wash*. Il. by Steven Kellogg. Dial, 1980.

Peet, Bill. *The Wump World*. Houghton, 1970.

Pinkwater, D. Manus. *Magic Camera*. Dodd, 1974.

——————. *The Big Orange Splot*. Hastings, 1977.

——————. *Pickle Creature*. Four Winds, 1979.

——————. *The Wuggie Norple Story*. Il. by Tomie de Paola. Four Winds, 1980.

Postma, Lidia. *The Witch's Garden*. McGraw-Hill, 1979.

Quin-Harkin, Janet. *Magic Growing Powder*. Il. by Art Cumings. Parent's, 1981.

Raskin, Ellen. *Ghost in a Four-Room Apartment*. Atheneum, 1974.

Reavin, Sam. *Hurray for Captain Jane!* Il. by Emily Arnold McCully. Parent's, 1971.

Sendak, Maurice. *In the Night Kitchen*. Harper & Row, 1970.

Sharmat, Marjorie Weinman. *What Are We Going to Do About Andrew?* Il. by Ray Cruz. Macmillan, 1980.

Sleator, William. *Once, Said Darlene*. Il. by Steven Kellogg. Dutton, 1979.

Spier, Peter. *Bored — Nothing To Do!* Doubleday, 1978.

Stevenson, James. *The Wish Card Ran Out!* Greenwillow, 1981.

Tapio, Pat Decker. *The Lady Who Saw the Good Side of Everything*. Il. by Paul Galdone. Seabury, 1975.

Thayer, Jane. *Applebaum's Have a Robot*. Il. by Bari Weissman. Morrow, 1980.

Turkle, Brinton. *Do Not Open*. Dutton, 1981.

Van Allsburg, Chris. *The Garden of Adbul Gasazi*. Houghton, 1979.

——————. *Jumanji*. Houghton, 1981.

Waber, Bernard. *You're a Little Kid With a Big Heart*. Houghton, 1980.

Zimelman, Nathan. *If I Were Strong Enough*. Il. by Diane Paterson. Abingdon, 1982.

Animal Fantasy

Three mini-centers are suggested in this section: 1) " 'Pig Out' On A Good Book" (books about pigs); 2) "A Bear Everywhere" (books about bears); and 3) "Be Nice to Mice" (books about mice). A bibliography follows the description of each center. A bibliography of fantasy books dealing with a variety of animals is included at the end of this chapter.

BOOKS ABOUT PIGS

A bulletin board forms the backdrop for this mini-center:

Have as many books about pigs as possible available in the center.

1) **Readiness activity.** The "Dress the Pigs" activity based on *Mr. and Mrs. Pig's Evening Out* by Mary Rayner develops skill in color and texture recognition and in following simple directions .Make *two* of the pigs shown on the next page from laminated posterboard. Cut dresses for Mrs. Pig from poster board using the pattern on page 70. Also using the dress pattern, make five dresses from materials of varying textures. Glue the material onto the pos - terboard dresses. Suggested materials: corduroy ,burlap, terry cloth, velvet, and satin. Make

Pattern for Mr. and Mrs. Pig

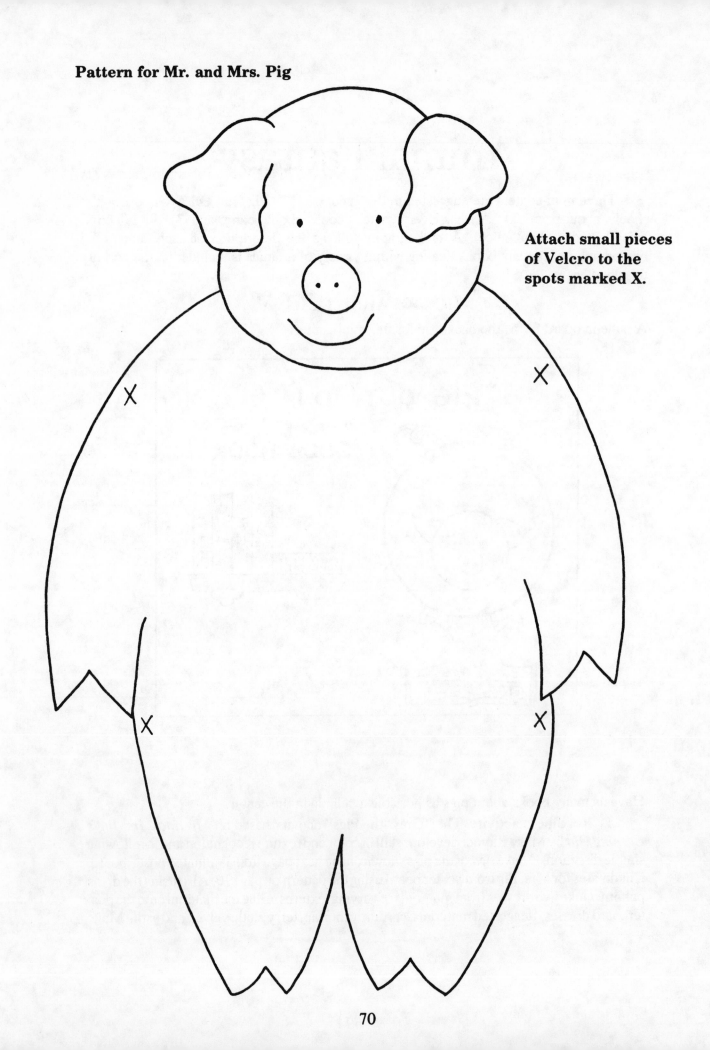

Attach small pieces of Velcro to the spots marked X.

Pattern for dress for Mrs. Pig.

Attach small pieces of Velcro to the *back* of each dress on the spots marked X.

You may want to decorate the different dresses with bits of ribbon, trim, or buttons.

Patterns for clothing for Mr. Pig.

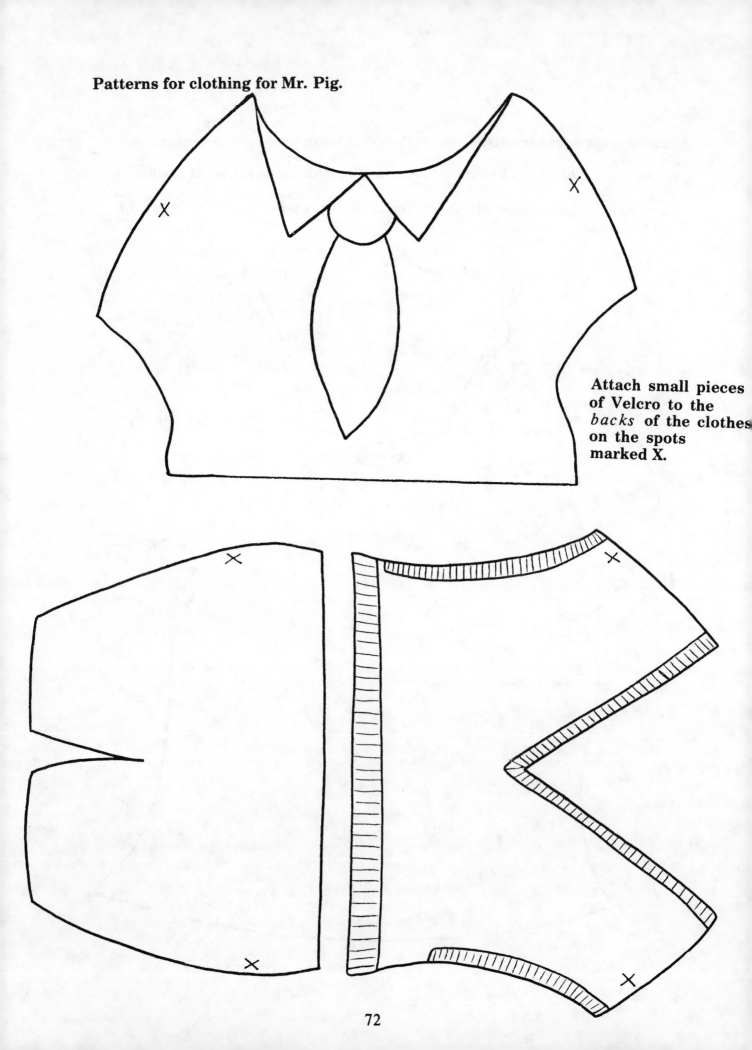

Attach small pieces
of Velcro to the
backs of the clothes
on the spots
marked X.

72

posterboard patterns of the clothing for Mr. Pig. Glue felt on the posterboard. Cut two pairs of pants and two shirts in different colors and one vest. Prepare this set of directions for Mrs. Pig:

Dress Mrs. Pig for the evening out.
1. Give [pig] the [shirt] to wear.
2. Give [pig] the [shirt] to wear.
3. Give [pig] the [shirt] to wear.
4. Give [pig] the [shirt] to wear.
5. Give [pig] the [shirt] to wear.

Each of these symbols should be cut from the *same* material from which the dresses are made.

Prepare this set of directions for Mr. Pig:

Dress Mr. Pig for the evening out.
1. Give [pig] a blue [shirt] to wear.
2. Give [pig] red [pants] to wear.
3. Give [pig] a yellow [shirt] to wear.
4. Give [pig] green [pants] to wear.
5. Give [pig] an orange [vest] to wear.

Mr. Pig's clothes may or may not be color coded, depending on the needs of individual groups of children.

2) **Pig Paper Bag Puppets.** Have the children make pig paper bag puppets, using the pattern on page 76. Children could pick a favorite pig story and do a puppet dramatization of a scene from it. Glue the head of the pig on the "flap." Glue the mouth under the flap onto the bag as shown on the next page, gluing the top of the mouth to the underside of the flap as shown.

 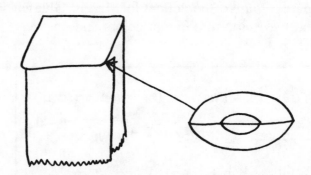

3) **Sequencing activity.** Using James Marshall's *Yummers* as a stimulus, have the children put in order all the foods that Emily Pig ate when she went for a walk. Make picture cards (3 x 4 inches) of these foods: sandwich; corn on the cob; scones; Eskimo pies; Girl Scout cookies; malt; banana split; peach ice cream; pizza; cherry pop and candied apple. Number the cards on the back for self-checking. Have the book available for the children to use.

4) **Mural.** Have the children make a mural of *The Pig's Wedding* by Helme Heine. Let the children make a background for the mural. Then, since the pigs in the story paint their clothing, have each child paint a pig to attend the wedding. Cut out all the pigs and glue them to the background. Don't forget the bride and groom.

5) **Creative writing.** Display children's stories under the heading "Pig Tales." A starter list of story ideas is given below. Teachers will want to add other ideas to this list.

a. After reading any of the the Rayner books (*Mr. and Mrs. Pig's Evening Out, Garth Pig and the Ice Cream Lady*, or *Mrs. Pig's Bulk Buy*) write an adventure for Garth Pig or another one of the pig brothers or sisters.

b. After reading *Hooray for Pig!* by Carla Stevens, write something that was hard for *you* to learn to do. (Pig had a difficult time learning to swim.)

c. The *Paddy Pork* books by John Goodall are wordless. Write a story to accompany the pictures. Write another adventure for Paddy and illustrate it.

d. After reading *The Piggy in the Puddle* by Pomerantz and *This Little Pig-A-Wig and Other Rhymes about Pigs* by the Blevgads, write a pig rhyme of two or three lines and make a picture of your pig. (The teacher can put all of these rhymes and illustrations together to make a class book.)

e. After reading *Pig Pig Grows Up* by David McPhail, write a story about some things that you used to do when you were small that you do not do now.

SELECTED BIBLIOGRAPHY OF BOOKS ABOUT PIGS

Blevgad, Lenore. *This Little Pig-A-Wig and Other Rhymes About Pigs*. Il. by Erik Blevgad. Atheneum, 1978.

Bond, Felicia. *Mary Betty Lizzie McNutt's Birthday*. Crowell, 1983.

_____. *Poinsettia & Her Family*. Crowell, 1981.

Boynton, Sandra. *Hester in the Wild*. Harper & Row, 1979.

Cole, Brock. *Nothing But a Pig*. Doubleday, 1981.

Gackenbach, Dick. *The Pig Who Saw Everything*. Seabury, 1978.

Getz, Arthur. *Humphrey the Dancing Pig*. Dial, 1980.

Goodall, John. *The Adventures of Paddy Pork*. Harcourt, 1968.

_____. *The Ballooning Adventures of Paddy Pork*. Harcourt, 1969.

_____. *Paddy's Evening Out*. Atheneum, 1973.

_____. *Paddy Pork's Holiday*. Atheneum, 1976.

_____. *Paddy's New Hat*. Atheneum, 1980.

_____. *Paddy Goes Traveling*. Atheneum, 1982.

Heine, Helme. *The Pig's Wedding*. Atheneum, 1979.

Hoban, Lillian. *Mr. Pig and Family*. Harper & Row, 1980.

Jeschke, Susan. *Perfect the Pig*. Holt, 1981.

King-Smith, Dick. *Pigs Might Fly*. Il. by Mary Rayner. Viking, 1982.

Lampell, Mildred. *The Pig With One Nostril*. Il. by Peter Parnall. Doubleday, 1975.

Lobel, Arnold. *The Book of Pigricks*. Harper & Row, 1983.

_____. *Small Pig*. Harper & Row, 1969.

Marshall, James. *Yummers*. Houghton, 1973.

_____. *Portly McSwine*. Houghton, 1979.

McClenathan, Louise. *The Easter Pig*. Il. by Rosekrans Hoffman. Morrow, 1982.

McPhail, David. *Pig Grows Up*. Dutton, 1980.

_____. *Pig Pig Rides*. Dutton, 1982.

Miles, Miska. *This Little Pig*. Il. by Leslie Morrill. Dutton, 1980.

Murphy, Jim. *Harold Thinks Big*. Il. by Susanna Natti. Crown, 1980.

Oxenbury, Helen. *Pig Tale*. Morrow, 1973.

Peck, Robert Newton. *Hamilton*. Il. by Laura Lydecker. Little, Brown, 1976.

Peet, Bill. *Chester the Worldly Pig*. Houghton, 1965.

Pinkwater, D. Manus. *Three Big Hogs*. Seabury, 1975.

Pomerantz, Charlotte. *The Piggy in the Puddle*. Il. by James Marshall. Macmillan, 1974.

Rayner, Mary. *Mr. and Mrs. Pig's Evening Out*. Atheneum, 1976.

_____. *Garth Pig and the Ice Cream Lady*. Atheneum, 1977.

_____. *Mrs. Pig's Bulk Buy*. Atheneum, 1981.

Steig, William. *Roland the Minstrel Pig*. Windmill, 1968.

_____. *Farmer Palmer's Wagon Ride*. Farrar, 1974.

_____. *The Amazing Bone*. Farrar, 1976.

Stevens, Carla. *Horray for Pig*. Il. by Rainey Bennett. Scholastic, 1974.

Stine, Jovial Bob. *The Pigs' Book of World Records*. Il. by Peter Lippman. Random, 1980.

Ungerer, Tomi. *The Mellops go Diving for Treasure*. Harper & Row, 1957.

Van Leeuwen, Jean. *Tales of Oliver Pig*. Il. by Arnold Lobel. Dial, 1981.

_____. *More Tales of Oliver Pig*. Il. by Arnold Lobel. Dial, 1981.

_____. *Amanda Pig and Her Brother Oliver*. Il. by Ann Schweninger. Dial, 1982.

Winthrop, Elizabeth. *Sloppy Kisses*. Il. by Anne Burgess. Macmillan 1980.

Pattern for Pig Paper Bag Puppet

Cut *two* **of the mouth sections.**

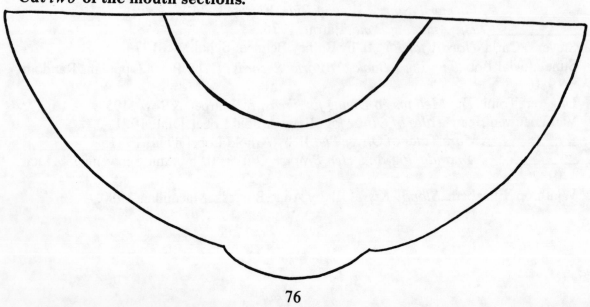

BOOKS ABOUT BEARS

Have as many books with bears as characters as possible in the center. The backdrop for this mini-center is a bulletin board made by the children. The bulletin board is based on the book *Bears* by Ruth Krauss. In the book, bears are shown "everywheres" — on the stairs, under chairs, etc. Title the bulletin board "A BEAR EVERYWHERE" and have each child make a bear. Let the class decide what else they need for the board and where to put the bears. Activities:

1) **Creative dramatization.** Using *Bear Circus* by Williem Pene du Bois and *The Bear on the Motorcycle* by Reiner Zimnik for ideas, have the children plan and dramatize circus acts. Include individual acts and group acts and a ringmaster. Keep costuming and props to a minimum. Emphasize the *planning* aspect by having the children decide what they will do and how they will carry it out.

2) **Choral reading and pantomine.** *Bear Winter* by Lillie Chaffin lends itself well to this type of activity. The book has a rhymed text and a repeated refrain on every page:

> "But the big brown bear
> And the small brown bear
> Just didn't care.
> They didn't care at all, at all;
> They didn't care at all."

The teacher could read the text, and the children could read the refrain each time that it occurs. The story tells of a mother and baby brown bear's hibernating all winter and waking in the spring. There are several scenes in the book that could be pantomimed:

— the bears, curled up, fast asleep
— the bears, yawning and stretching, just waking up
— mother bear, brushing dry leaves from baby's fur
— baby bear, hesitantly following mother bear out of the den
— the bears lifting their heads, standing on toes, twitching noses
— the bears tasting honey

3) **Making predictions/Critical reading.** James Marshall's *What's the Matter with Carruthers?* invites the children to answer the question posed by the title. The book builds incident upon incident of the two friends' trying everything to make the usually good-natured Carruthers happy. Winter is clearly approaching in the book, but the author does not reveal until the end why Carruthers is behaving as he is. A follow-up to the reading of this book could

be to have the children make a chart of things they could do to cheer up someone. They can compare their chart with the things Carruthers' friends did in the book.

4) **"Bear" vocabulary.** The children are to match words having to do with bears with their definitions. Make these cards to go with the electric board described in Chapter 2:

DON'T BE EM-BEAR-RASSED!
LEARN THESE WORDS

cub	The place where a bear sleeps.
hibernate	A black and white bear.
den	A bear uses these to help him climb.
koala	A white bear that likes cold and snow.
panda	A baby bear.
honey	What a bear does in the winter.
paws	A real teddy bear that lives in Australia.
grizzly	A food bears like to eat.
polar	A big brown bear that may be dangerous.

5) **Skills activity — initial consonant "b."** This visual discrimination activity is for kindergarten and first grade. Make the bulletin board shown on the next page. Make a set of word cards in which some of the words begin with "b" and the rest begin with other consonants. Include the words that begin with "d," "p," "q," "g," consonants that are frequently confused with "b." Children are to sort the word cards into two sets: those that begin with "b" and all others. They are to put the "b" words into the honey pot and the other words into the hive. Picture code for self-checking by putting a bee on the back of the "b" word cards and honeypot on the back of the other word cards.

Sample cards (actual size): front   back

6) **Skills activity — homonyms.** This activity is intended for second and third grade. Use the same bulletin board shown on the next page. Change the title to "BEAR OR BARE." Keep all the homonyms cards (example shown below) in the large honey pot on the board. Children are to read the sentences on the cards, select the correct homonym by putting their pencil through the hole, and self-check by turning the card over to see if their pencil is through the marked hole. They then return all homonym cards to the honey pot.

Bulletin Board

Use the bear for both skills activities
described on the preceding page.

Sample homonym card (actual size):

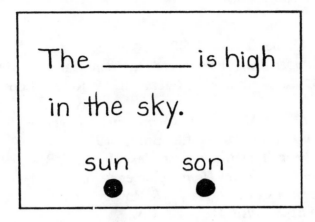

7) Crossword puzzle. The puzzle is based on the book *Milton the Early Riser* by Robert Kraus. Have the book available for the children to use if needed.

SELECTED BIBLIOGRAPHY OF BOOKS ABOUT BEARS

Asch, Frank. *Moon Bear*. Scribner, 1978.

_____. *Sand Cake*. Parent's, 1979.

_____. *Happy Birthday, Moon*. Prentice-Hall, 1982.

_____. *Milk and Cookies*. Parent's, 1982.

Bach, Alice. *The Smartest Bear and His Brother Oliver*. Il. by Steven Kellogg. Harper & Row, 1975.

_____. *The Most Delicious Camping Trip Ever*. Il. by Steven Kellogg. Harper & Row, 1976.

_____. *Millicent the Magnificent*. Il. by Steven Kellogg. Harper & Row, 1978.

Browne, Anthony. *Bear Hunt*. Antheneum, 1979.

Bunting, Eve. *The Valentine Bears*. Il by Jan Brett. Houghton/Clarion, 1983.

Cartlidge, Michelle. *The Bear's Bazaar*. Lothrop, 1979.

Chaffin, Lillie D. *Bear Weather*. Il. by Helga Aichinger. Macmillan, 1969.

Dabcovich, Lydia. *Sleepy Bear*. Dutton, 1982.

Delton, Judy. *Brimhall Turns to Magic*. Il. by Bruce Degan. Lothrop, 1979.

Duvoisin, Roger. *Snowy and Woody*. Knopf, 1979.

Freeman, Don. *Bearymore*. Viking, 1976.

Gackenbach, Dick. *The Adventures of Albert, The Running Bear*. Clarion, 1982.

Gammell, Stephen. *Wake Up, Bear . . . It's Christmas!* Lothrop, 1981.

Ginsburg, Mirra. *Two Greedy Bears*. Il. by Jose Aruego and Ariane Dewey. Macmillan, 1976.

Gordon, Margaret. *Wilberforce Goes on a Picnic*. Morrow, 1982.

Hale, Irina. *Brown Bear in a Brown Chair*. Atheneum, 1983.

Hayes, Gregory. *Bear by Himself*. Harper & Row, 1976.

Hellsing, Lennart. *The Wonderful Pumpkin*. Il. by Svend Otto. Atheneum, 1976.

Hodgson, Ila. *Bernadette's Busy Morning*. Il. by John Johnson. Parent's, 1968.

Kraus, Robert. *Milton the Early Riser*. Il. by Jose Aruego and Ariane Dewey. Windmill, 1972.

Krauss, Ruth. *Bears*. Harper & Row, 1948.

Lipkind, William. *Number Bear*. Il. by Roger Duvoisin. Harcourt, 1966.

Margolis, Richard J. *Big Bear to the Rescue*. Il. by Robert Lopshire. Greenwillow, 1975.

Marshall, James. *What's the Matter with Carruthers?* Houghton, 1972.

McPhail, David. *Henry Bear's Park*. Little, Brown, 1976.

Minarik, Else. *Little Bear*. Il. by Maurice Sendak. Harper & Row, 1957.

_____. *Father Bear Comes Home*. Harper & Row.

_____. *Little Bear's Friend*. Harper & Row.

_____. *Little Bear's Visit*. Harper & Row.

_____. *A Kiss for Little Bear*. Harper & Row.

Murphy, Jill. *Peace at Last*. Dial, 1980.

Parker, Nancy Winslow. *The Ordeal of Byron B. Blackbear*. Dodd, 1979.

Peet, Bill. *Big Bad Bruce*. Houghton, 1977.

Pene du Bois, William. *Bear Circus*. Viking, 1971.

Pinkwater, D. Manus. *Bear's Picture*. Holt, 1972.

Ruck-Pauquet, Gina. *Mumble Bear*. Trans. by Anthea Bell. Il. by Erika Dietzsch-Capelle. Putnam, 1980.

Steiner, Jorg. *The Bear Who Wanted to be a Bear*. Il. by Jorg Muller. Antheneum, 1977.

Stevenson, James. *The Bear Who Had No Place To Go*. Harper & Row, 1972.

Turkle, Brinton. *Deep in the Forest*. Dutton, 1976.

Wahl, Jan. *Sylvester Bear Overslept*. Il. by Lee Lorenz. Parent's, 1979.

Ward, Andrew. *Baby Bear and the Long Sleep*. Il. by John Walsh. Little, Brown, 1980.

Watanabe, Shigeo. *What a Good Lunch*. Il. by Yasuo Ohtomo. Collins, 1980.

_____. *Get Set! Go!*. Il. by Yasuo Ohtomo. Philomel, 1981.

_____. *Where's My Daddy?* Il. by Yasuo Ohtomo. Putnam, 1982.

_____. *I Can Ride It!* Il. by Yasuo Ohtomo. Putnam, 1982.

_____. *I'm King of the Castle*. Il. by Yasuo Ohtomo. Putnam, 1982.

Weisl, Lisl. *Gertie and Gus*. Parent's, 1977.

Weinberg, Lawrence. *The Forgetful Bears*. Il. by Paula Winter. Houghton/Clarion, 1982.

Wildsmith, Brian. *Bear's Adventure*. Random, 1982.

Winter, Paula. *The Bear and the Fly*. Crown, 1976.

Zimnik, Reiner. *The Bear on the Motorcycle*. Atheneum, 1970.

Children might enjoy having these longer books read aloud to them:

Haas, Dorothy. *The Bears Upstairs*. Greenwillow, 1978.

Wilson, Gahan. *Harry the Fat Bear Spy*. Scribner, 1973.

Since many young children have teddy bears, they might enjoy some of these books about toy bears:

Binzen, Bill. *Alfred Goes Flying*. Doubleday, 1976.

Boegehold, Betty. *Bear Underground*. Il. by Jim Arnosky. Doubleday, 1980.

Dillon, Barbara. *Who Needs a Bear?* Il. by Diane de Groat. Morrow, 1981.

Flora, James. *Sherwood Walks Home*. Harcourt, 1966.

Freeman, Don. *Corduroy*. Viking, 1968.

_____. *A Pocket for Corduroy*. Viking, 1978.

Gretz, Susanna. *Teddy Bears' Moving Day*. Four Winds, 1981.

_____. *Teddy Bears Go Shopping*. Four Winds, 1982.

Kantrowitz, Mildred. *Willy Bear*. Il. by Nancy Winslow Parker. Parent's, 1976.

Nakatani, Chiyoko. *My Teddy Bear*. Crowell, 1976.

Read alouds:

Howe, Deborah and James. *Teddy Bear's Scrapbook*. Il. by David Rose. Atheneum, 1980.

Milne, A.A. *Winnie the Pooh*. Dutton, 1926.

Read *Milton the Early Riser* by Robert Kraus.
Read the sentences below. Find the missing words.
Use the words at the bottom of the page to help you.
Then write the words in the puzzle.

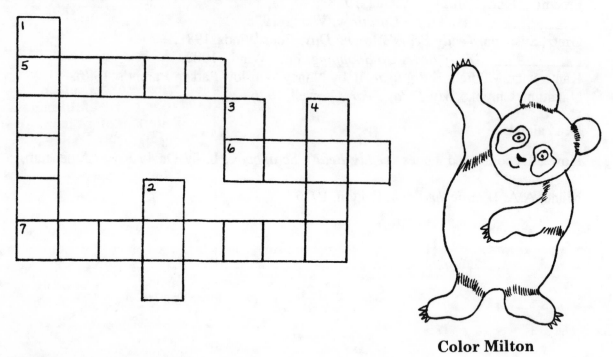

Color Milton

DOWN

1. Milton did _____.
2. A wind blew the sleepers out of _____.
3. When everyone woke _____, Milton fell asleep.
4. Milton _____ and danced.

ACROSS

5. Milton was an early _____.
6. Milton had no one to _____ with.
7. Everyone was _____.

riser   play   tricks   up

bed   sang   sleeping

84

BOOKS ABOUT MICE

The backdrop of this mini-center is the bulletin board shown below. Have as many books about mice as possible available for the children to read.

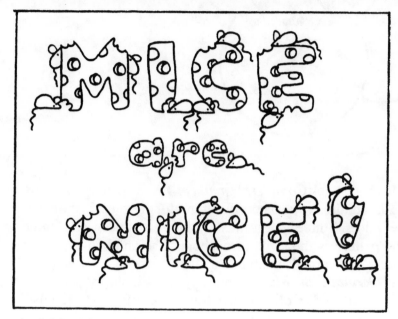

Make the letters from yellow construction paper to resemble cheese. Make the mice from gray construction paper.

Activities:

1) **Mouse Finger Puppets.** Children can make one or more of these finger puppets from construction paper. They can use their puppets to tell or dramatize their favorite mouse stories.

Glue a finger-size paper ring to the back of the finger puppet.

back

2) **Design-a-trap.** After reading *Whose Mouse Are You?* by Robert Kraus, have children design and build a mouse trap. Have available a variety of materials, such as boxes of different sizes, toothpicks, ice cream sticks, etc. Encourage the children to be as creative as they want.

3) **Shapes mouse.** For kindergarten and first grade, teach a lesson on shapes and make this construction paper mouse. A large circle, two small circles, and a triangle are needed. To make the mouse, paste the triangle onto the large circle as shown. Then paste the two small circles on the two corners of the triangle. Add construction paper eyes, whiskers, and a tail.

4) **Mouse Adventures.** Using the book *Complete Version of Ye Three Blind Mice* by John Ivimey as a stimulus, have the children write other adventures for the mice. In the book, there are "verses" for "three cold mice," "three hungry mice," "three glad mice," and "three sick mice," among others. The pattern is the same throughout. The children can write additional verses using this pattern and compile them into a class book.

5) **Mouse Melodies.** Read *Geraldine the Music Mouse* by Leo Lionni and *Sylvester the Mouse with the Musical Ear* by Adelaide Holl to the children. Pick a tune that is familiar to the children, such as "Mary Had a Little Lamb," "Twinkle, Twinkle, Little Star," "Clementine," etc., and have them make up a song about a particular mouse or mice in general. Have them dictate the words for a language experience chart. Later, the song can be duplicated for every child to have a copy. If possible, provide appropriate accompaniment for the song, such a a flute (or a recorder) like Geraldine had, or a guitar, like Sylvester's.

6) **Bookmarks.** Provide children with the pattern below and have them make bookmarks. They will need to color them, cut them out, and attach a long piece of yarn for the tail.

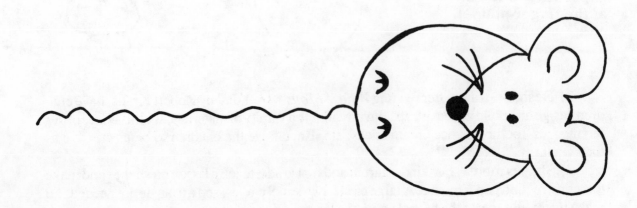

7) **Who-What-When-Where game — "Another Mouse to Feed."** This game, involving the classification of phrases into "who," "what," "when," and "where" categories, has as its theme the book *Another Mouse to Feed* by Robert Kraus. For this game, you will need a game board like the one shown on the next page, some pom pom mice, a box decorated like a trap to keep the mice in, and two sets of cards — phrase cards and "mouse" cards. The game board should be made from heavy duty poster board. The mice are made from 1½" gray pom poms. Trim one side of the pom down to a point for the nose. Cut out pink felt ears and glue in place. Glue on black bead eyes and a nose. Add a piece of gray yarn for the tail. The number of mice needed depends on the number of players. For three players, 12-15 mice are recommended. No particular type of box is needed, but it should have a lid so that it can be used for storage when the game is not in use. Listed below are suggested phrases for the phrase cards:

WHO	WHERE
a fire fighter	at the beach
the first grade teacher	in a tree
my friend	by the rock
the little boy	behind the chair
a brown-haired girl	under the bed
a football player	near the window
my mother	inside the box

WHAT	WHEN
a piece of cheese	yesterday
roller skates	in the morning
five dollars	after school
a box of cookies	before lunch
a new toy	all day
a funny book	on Saturday
some bubble gum	tomorrow

Teachers will want to add others to this list. Change the phrase cards used in this game often. Use the following suggested ideas for the "mouse" cards:

You just got a job delivering pizza. Put a mouse back in the trap.

You just won 1000 pounds of cheese in an eating contest. Put a mouse back in the trap.

You have been chosen to star in a movie with Mickey Mouse. Put a mouse back in the trap.

You have a stomach ache from eating too much cheese. Take one mouse from each of the other players.

A cat almost caught you, but you tricked him and got away. Put a mouse back in the trap.

You just won the tennis championship for mice. Put a mouse back in the trap.

You just lost your job at the car wash. Take a mouse from the trap.

The doctor put you on a diet — NO CHEESE! Take a mouse from the trap.

Use this as the model for a large game board

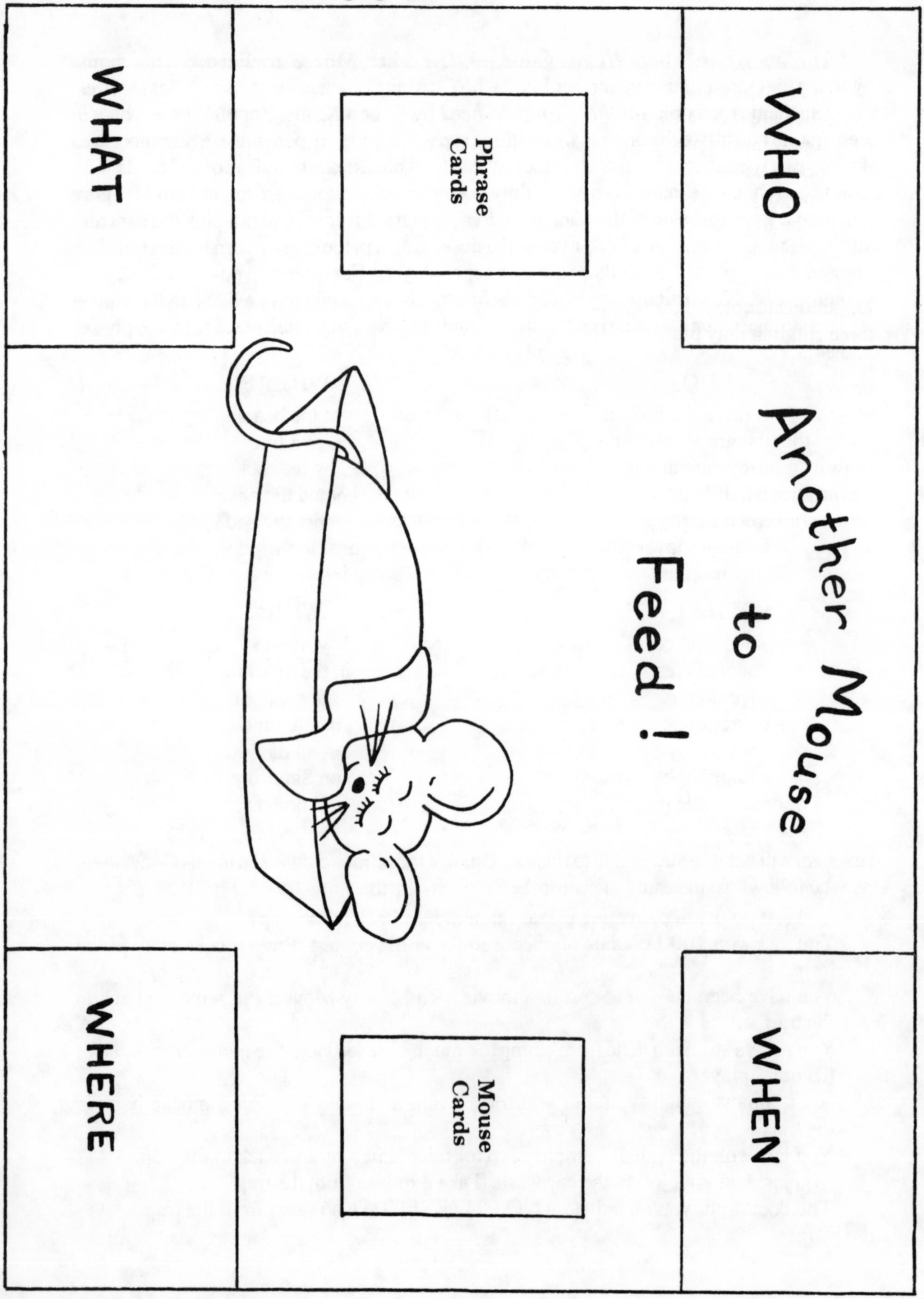

WHO

WHAT

Phrase
Cards

Another Mouse
to
Feed !

WHERE

WHEN

Mouse
Cards

You are going to be in the mouse roller derby. Practice your skating and put a mouse back in the trap.

Mice are nice! Put one of yours back in the trap.

A new family of mice just moved in next door. Share your cheese with them and put a mouse back in the trap.

You got your tail caught in a trap, but the other mice helped you get out. Put a mouse back in the trap.

You have been chosen to be the first mouse to go to the moon. Put a mouse back in the trap.

Directions for playing: Place phrase and "mouse" cards in the appropriate areas. Two or three children may play. Each player starts with three pom pom mice. A roll of a die determines who starts the game. The first player draws a phrase card and places it on one of the four areas on the board. If correct, he/she draws a "mouse" card. The player must read the card aloud and either take a mouse from the trap or put a mouse back in. Return used "mouse" cards to the bottom of the deck. If a player incorrectly classifies a phrase, he/she does not draw a "mouse" card and play proceeds to the next player. The game ends when one player has no mice left. If all phrase cards are used before one player gives up all his/her mice, pick up all the phrase cards, reshuffle them, and start the deck again. Scatter several "Another Mouse to Feed!" cards, as shown below, throughout the "mouse" card deck. when a player draws one of these special cards, he/she automatically takes a mouse from the trap.

SELECTED BIBLIOGRAPHY OF BOOKS ABOUT MICE

Balian, Lorna. *Mother's Mother's Day*. Abingdon, 1982.

Berson, Harold. *A Moose is Not a Mouse*. Crown, 1975.

Boegehold, Betty. *Pippa Mouse*. Il. by Cyndy Szekeres. Knopf, 1973.

_____. *Here's Pippa Again*. Il. by Cyndy Szekeres. Knopf, 1975.

_____. *Pippa Pops Out!* Il. by Cyndy Szekeres. Knopf, 1979.

_____. *Hurray for Pippa!* Il. by Cyndy Szekeres. Knopf, 1980.

Burningham, John. *Trubloff the Mouse Who Wanted to Play the Balalaika*. Random, 1964.

Cartlidge, Michelle. *A Mouse's Diary*. Lothrop, 1982.

Clifford, Sandy. *The Roquefort Gang*. Parnassus/Houghton, 1981.

Cunningham, Julia. *A Mouse Called Junction*. Il. by Michael Hague. Pantheon, 1980.

Delaney, Ned. *Two Strikes. Four Eyes*. Houghton, 1976.

Hall, Malcolm. *And Then the Mouse . . .* Il. by Stephen Gammell. Four Winds, 1980.

Hare, Norma Q. *Mystery at Mouse House*. Garrard, 1980.

Hoff, Syd. *Baseball Mouse*. Putnam, 1969.

Holl, Adelaide. *Moon Mouse*. Il. by Cyndy Szekeres. Random, 1969.

_____. *Sylvester the Mouse with the Musical Ear*. Il. by N.M. Bodecker. Golden, 1973.

Ivimey, John W. *Complete Version of Ye Three Blind Mice*. Il. by Walton Corbould. Warne, 1979.

Joerns, Consuelo. *The Foggy Rescue*. Four Winds, 1980.

Kelly, True and Steven Lindblom. *The Mouses' Terrible Christmas*. Lothrop, 1978.

Kraus, Robert. *Whose Mouse Are You?* Il. by Jose Aruego. Macmillan, 1970.

_____. *Pinchpenny Mouse*. Il. by Robert Byrd. Windmill, 1974.

_____. *Another Mouse to Feed*. Il. by Jose Aruego and Ariane Dewey. Windmill, 1980.

Kwitz, Mary DeBall. *Mouse at Home*. Harper & Row, 1966.

Lindblom, Steven. *The Mouses' Terrible Halloween*. Il. by True Kelley. Lothrop, 1980.

Lionni, Leo. *Frederick*. Pantheon, 1967.

_____. *Alexander and the Wind-Up Mouse*. Pantheon, 1969.

_____. *Theodore and the Talking Mushroom*. Pantheon, 1971.

_____. *The Greentail Mouse*. Pantheon, 1973.

_____. *Geraldine the Music Mouse*. Pantheon, 1979.

Lobel, Arnold. *Mouse Tales*. Harper & Row, 1972.

_____. *Mouse Soup*. Harper & Row, 1977.

Massie, Diane Redfield. *Zigger Beans*. Parent's, 1971.

Miles, Miska. *Mouse Six and the Happy Birthday*. Il. by Leslie Morrill. Dutton, 1978.

Miller, Edna. *Mousekin's Golden House*. Prentice-Hall, 1964.

_____. *Mousekin's Christmas Eve*. Prentice-Hall, 1967.

_____. *Mousekin Finds a Friend*. Prentice-Hall, 1967.

_____. *Mousekin's Woodland Sleepers*. Prentice-Hall, 1970.

_____. *Mousekin's Fables*. Prentice-Hall, 1982.

Nixon, Joan Lowery. *Muffie Mouse and the Busy Birthday*. Il. by Geoffrey Hayes. Seabury, 1978.

Oakley, Graham. *The Church Mice and the Moon*. Atheneum, 1974.

_____. *The Church Mice Adrift*. Atheneum, 1976.

_____. *The Church Mice in Action*. Atheneum, 1983.

_____. *The Church Mice Spread Their Wings*. Atheneum, 1976.

_____. *The Church Mice at Bay*. Atheneum, 1979.

_____. *The Church Mice at Christmas*. Atheneum, 1980.

Peppe, Rodney. *The Mice Who Lived in a Shoe*. Lothrop, 1982.

Polushkin, Maria. *Mother, Mother, I Want Another*. Il. by Diane Dawson.

Potter, Beatrix. *The Tale of Two Bad Mice*. Warne, 1904.

_____. *The Tale of Mrs. Tittlemouse*. Warne, 1910.

_____. *The Tale of Johnny Town-Mouse*. Warne, 1918.

Sampson, Pamela. *The Incredible Invention of Alexander Woodmouse*. Rand McNally, 1982.

Sharmet, Marjorie W. *Twitchell the Wishful*. Il. by Janet Stevens. Holiday, 1981.

Soule, Jean and Nancy. *Scuttle, the Stowaway Mouse*. Il. by Barbara Remington. Parent's, 1969.

Titus, Eve. *Anatole*. Il. by Paul Galdone. McGraw-Hill, 1956.

   (also: *Anatole and the Cat, Anatole and the Robot, Anatole Over Paris, Anatole and the Poodle, Anatole and the Piano, Anatole and the Thirty Thieves, Anatole and the Toyshop, Anatole in Italy,* and *Anatole and the Pied Piper*.)

Udry, Janice May. *Thump and Plunk*. Il. by Ann Schweninger. Harper & Row, 1981.

Watson, Clyde. *How Brown Mouse Kept Christmas*. Il. by Wendy Watson. Farrar, 1980.

Wenning, Elizabeth. *The Christmas Mouse*. Il. by Barbara Remington. Holt, 1959.

Wilbur, Richard. *Loud Mouse*. Il. by Don Almquist. Harcourt, 1982.

Yeoman, John. *Mouse Trouble*. Il. by Quentin Blake. Macmillan, 1972.

Yolen, Jane. *Mice on Ice*. Il. by Laurence Di Fiori. Dutton, 1980.

Read alouds:

Cleary, Beverly. *The Mouse and the Motorcycle*. Morrow, 1965.

_____. *Runaway Ralph*. Morrow, 1970.

_____. *Ralph S. Mouse*. Morrow, 1982.

Drury, Roger. *The Champion of Merrimack County*. Little, Brown, 1976.

Freschet, Berniece. *Bernard Sees the World*. Il. by Gina Freschet. Scribner, 1976.

_____. *Bernard of Scotland Yard*. Il. by Gina Freschet. Scribner, 1978.

_____. *Bernard and the Catnip Caper*. Il. by Gina Freschet. Scribner, 1981.

Hoban, Lillian. *It's Really Christmas*. Greenwillow, 1982.

Hoban, Russell. *The Mouse and His Child*. Il. by Lillian Hoban. Harper, 1967.

Lawson, Robert. *Ben and Me*. Little, Brown, 1939.

Sharp, Margery. The *Miss Bianca* series. Little, Brown.

Selden, George. *Tucker's Countryside*. Il. by Garth Williams. Farrar, 1969.

Van Leeuwen, Jean. *The Great Cheese Conspiracy*. Il by Imero Gobbato. Dell, 1973.

_____. *The Great Christmas Kidnapping Caper*. Il. by Steven Kellogg. Dial, 1975.

_____. *The Great Rescue Operation*. Il by Margot Apple. Dial, 1982.

SELECTED BIBLIOGRAPHY OF ANIMAL FANTASY

Adams, Adrienne. *The Easter Egg Artists*. Scribner, 1976 (rabbits)

Allard, Harry. *I Will Not Go to Market Today*. Il. by James Marshall. Dial, 1979.

Allen, Jeffrey. *Mary Alice, Operator Number 9*. Il. by James Marshall. Little, Brown, 1975. (duck)

Asch, Frank. *MacGoose's Grocery*. Il. by James Marshall. Dial, 1978.

Baker, Alan. *Benjamin's Book*. Lothrop, 1983.

Brown, Marc. *Arthur's April Fool*. Little, Brown, 1983. (aardvark)

_____. *Arthur's Nose*. Little, Brown, 1976.

_____. *Arthur's Eyes*. Little, Brown, 1979.

_____. *Arthur Goes to Camp*. Little, Brown, 1982.

Calhoun, Mary. *Cross-Country Cat* Il. by Erick Ingraham. Morrow, 1979.

Carrick, Malcolm. *Mr. Tod's Trap*. Harper & Row, 1980 (fox)

Cazet, Denys. *Lucky Me*. Bradbury, 1983. (chicken)

Chorao, Kay. *Maudie's Umbrella*. Dutton, 1975.

Clymer, Eleanor. *Horatio's Birthday*. Il. by Robert Quackenbush. Atheneum, 1976. (cat)

_____. *Horatio Goes to the Country*. Il. by Robert Quackenbush. Atheneum, 1978.

Crowe, Robert. *Tyler Toad and the Thunder*. Il. by Kay Chorao. Dutton, 1980.

Delton, Judy. *Three Friends Find Spring*. Il. by Guilio Maestro. Crown, 1977.

_____. *The Goose Who Wrote a Book*. Il. by Catherine Cleary. Carolrhoda, 1982.

Demarest, Chris. *Benedict Finds a Home*. Lothrop, 1982. (bird)

de Paola, Tomie. *Bill and Pete*. Putnam, 1978. (crocodile)

Ernst, Kathryn. *Owl's New Cards*. Il. by Diane de Groat. Crown, 1977.

Flory, Jane. *We'll Have a Friend for Lunch*. Il. by Carolyn Croll. Houghton, 1974. (cat)

Freeman, Don. *Dandelion*. Viking, 1964. (lion)

Gackenbach, Dick. *Claude and Pepper*. Seabury, 1976. (dogs)

Gantos, Jack. *Rotten Ralph*. Il. by Nicole Rubel. Houghton, 1976. (cat)

_____. *Worse than Rotten Ralph*. Il. by Nicol Rubel. Houghton, 1978.

Ginsburg, Mirra. *The Chick and the Duckling*. Il. by Jose and Ariane Aruego. Macmillan, 1972.

_____. *Mushroom in the Rain*. Il. by Jose and Ariane Aruego. Macmillan, 1974.

Griffith, Helen V. *Alex and the Cat*. Il. by Joseph Low. Greenwillow, 1982. (dog)

Heine, Helma. *Friends*. Atheneum, 1982. (rooster, mouse, pig)

Hoban, Lillian. *Arthur's Christmas Cookies*. Harper & Row 1972. (monkey)

_____. *Arthur's Honey Bear*. Harper & Row, 1974.

_____. *Arthur's Pen Pal*. Harper & Row, 1976.

_____. *Arthur's Prize Reader*. Harper & Row, 1978.

_____. *Arthur's Funny Money*. Harper & Row, 1981.

_____. *Harry's Song*. Greenwillow, 1978. (rabbit)

Hoban, Russell. *Bedtime for Frances*. Il. by Lillian Hoban. Harper & Row, 1960. (badger)

    (also *A Baby Sister for Frances, Bread and Jam for Frances, A Birthday for Frances, Best Friends for Frances,* and *A Bargain for Frances*.)

Hoban, Russell. *Harvey's Hideout*. Il. by Lillian Hoban. Parent's, 1969.

_____. *Dinner at Alberta's*. Il. by James Marshall. Crowell, 1975.

Hoffman, Rosekrans. *Anna Banana*. Knopf, 1975. (monkey)

Hogrogian, Nonny. *Carrot Cake*. Greenwillow, 1977. (rabbit)

Hutchins, Pat. *The Surprise Birthday*. Macmillan, 1969.

_____. *Good Night, Owl!* Macmillan, 1972.

Jeschke, Susan. *Sidney*. Holt, 1975. (chick)

Kessler, Leonard. *Old Turtle's Baseball Stories*. Greenwillow, 1982.

Kraus, Robert. *Leo the Late Bloomer*. Il. by Jose Aruego. Windmill, 1971. (tiger)

_____. *Owliver*. Il. by Jose Aruego and Ariane Dewey. Windmill, 1974. (owl)

_____. *Herman the Helper*. Il. by Jose Aruego and Ariane Dewey. Windmill, 1974. (octopus)

_____. *Three Friends*. Il. by Jose Aruego and Ariane Dewey. Windmill, 1975.

_____. *Boris Bad Enough*. Il. by Jose Aruego and Ariane Dewey. Dutton, 1976. (elephant)

_____. *Noel the Coward*. Il. by Jose Aruego and Ariane Dewey. Windmill, 1977. (kangaroo)

Kwitz, Mary DeBall. *Little Chick's Big Day*. Il. by Bruce Degan. Harper & Row, 1981.

Lobel, Arnold. *Frog and Toad are Friends*. Harper & Row, 1970.

_____. *Frog and Toad Together*. Harper & Row, 1972.

_____. *Frog and Toad All Year*. Harper & Row, 1976.

_____. *Days with Frog and Toad*. Harper & Row, 1979.

_____. *Owl at Home*. Harper & Row, 1975.

_____. *Uncle Elephant*. Harper & Row, 1981.

Marshall, Edward. *Fox and His Friends*. Il. by James Marshall. Dial, 1982.

_____. *Fox at School*. Il. by James Marshall. Dial, 1983.

_____. *Fox in Love*. Il. by James Marshall. Dial, 1982.

Marshall, James. *George and Martha*. Houghton, 1972. (hippopotamus)

_____. *George and Martha Encore*. Houghton, 1973.

_____. *George and Martha Rise and Shine*. Houghton, 1976.

_____. *George and Martha One Fine Day*. Houghton, 1978.

_____. *George and Martha Tons of Fun*. Houghton, 1980.

_____. *The Guest*. Houghton, 1975. (moose)

Massie, Diane Redfield. *Dazzle*. Parent's, 1969. (peacock)

McPhail, David. *Where Can an Elephant Hide?* Doubleday, 1979.

Meddaugh, Susan. *Maude and Claude Go Abroad*. Houghton, 1980. (fox)

Oakley, Graham. *Hetty and Harriet*. Atheneum, 1982. (hens)

Panek, Dennis. *Matilda Hippo Has a Big Mouth*. Bradbury, 1980.

_____. *Detective Whoo*. Bradbury, 1981. (owl)

Peet, Bill. *How Droofus the Dragon Lost His Head*. Houghton, 1971.

_____. *The Gnats of Knotty Pine*. Houghton, 1975.

_____. *Cyrus the Unsinkable Sea Serpent*. Houghton, 1975.

_____. *Eli*. Houghton, 1978. (lion)

_____. *Cowardly Clyde*. Houghton, 1979.

Preston, Edna Mitchell. *Where Did My Mother Go?* Il .by Chris Conover. Four Winds, 1978. (cat)

Roy, Ron .*Three Ducks Went Wandering*. Il. by Paul Galdone. Seabury, 1979.

Selden, George. *Chester Cricket's Pigeon Ride*. Il. by Garth Williams. Farrar, 1981.

Shannon, George .*Dance Away*. Il. by Jose Aruego and Ariane Dewey. Greenwillow, 1982. (rabbits)

Sharmat, Marjorie Weinman. *Sophie and Gussie*. Il. by Lillian Hoban. Macmillan, 1973.

_____. *Griselda's New Year*. Il. by Norman Chartier. Macmillan, 1979. (goose)

Sharmat, Mitchell. *Gregory the Terrible Eater*. Il. by Jose Aruego and Ariene Dewey. Four Winds, 1980. (goat)

Steig, William. *Sylvester and the Magic Pebble*. Windmill, 1969. (donkey)

_____. *Tiffky Doofky*. Farrar, 1978. (dog)

_____. *Doctor Desoto*. Farrar, 1982. (mouse)

Steinmetz, Leon .*Pip Stories*. Little, Brown, 1980. (porcupine)

Stevenson, James. *Monty*. Greenwillow, 1979. (alligator)

_____. *Howard*. Greenwillow, 1980. (duck)

Thaler, Mike. *Owly*. Il. by David Weisner. Harper & Row, 1982. (owl)

Waber, Bernard. *"You Look Ridiculous," Said the Rhinoceros to the Hippopotamus*. Houghton, 1966.

_____. *An Anteater Named Arthur*. Houghton, 1967.

_____. *A Firefly Named Torchy*. Houghton, 1970.

_____. *I Was All Thumbs*. Houghton, 1975. (octopus)

_____. *Mice on My Mind*. Houghton, 1977. (cat)

Wahl, Jan. *Doctor Rabbit's Foundling*. Il. by Cyndy Szekeres. Pantheon, 1977.

_____. *Carrot Nose*. Il. by James Marshall. Farrar, 1978. (rabbit)

Wells, Rosemary. *Benjamin and Tulip*. Dial, 1973.

_____. *Stanley and Rhoda*. Dial, 1978.

_____. *Timothy Goes to School*. Dial, 1981.

Williams, Barbara. *Albert's Toothache*. Il. by Kay Chorao. Dutton, 1974. (turtle)

_____. *Chester Chipmunk's Thanksgiving*. Il. by Kay Chorao. Dutton, 1978.

Wittman, Sally. *Pelly and Peak*. Harper & Row, 1978. (pelican, peacock)

Zalben, Jane Breskin. *Penny and the Captain*. Collins World, 1978. (penguin)

_____. *Porcupine's Christmas Blues*. Philomel, 1982.

CHAPTER FIVE

Exceptional Children

With the implementation of federal legislation entitling children with special needs to participate in regular educational programs, there came a need to provide children and teachers with information regarding handicapping conditions. In recent years, a great deal of children's literature dealing with exceptional children has been published. A number of these books are appropriate for primary grade children. The purpose of this chapter is to suggest books and activities that can be used to promote an awareness and an understanding of people who have a variety of handicaps.

Because of the nature of this topic and each classroom's unique situation, the suggestions offered here are for teacher-directed group activities. It is important that opportunities be provided for children to ask questions and to discuss both the content and the illustrations of the books.

These questions calling for critical thinking might serve as a basis for discussion of many of the books listed in this chapter:

1) What are some ways in which the handicapped character is different from you because of his/her handicap?

2) Are there any ways that the character is like you? What are they?

3) How do other people in the story feel about the handicapped character?

4) What kinds of things does the handicapped character do with his/her parents? Friends? Brothers and sisters? How do these activities compare with what you do with your parents/friends/brothers and sisters?

5) How do you feel about the story character? Would you like to have him/her for a friend? Why?

The teacher will probably need to introduce the specialized vocabulary in both the fiction and nonfiction books to the children. Unfamiliar words might be placed on a chart that will be kept in the classroom. As the teacher pronounces the words, children can offer their ideas as to the definitions. This activity is an excellent opportunity to find out what experiences and advance information the children have about the topic. As new books are shared, the chart can be referred to again and again to review terms and to speculate what related terms might appear in the book. For example, if the teacher tells the children that he/she will be reading a book about a blind child, they might predict, by looking at the chart, that the terms "Braille," "guide dog," "visually impaired" might also appear in the book. Add new vocabulary words to the chart periodically.

Activities:

1) To gain a greater understanding of deafness and an empathy for deaf persons, these books and activities may be helpful:

a. Two fictional stories, *Lisa and Her Soundless World* by Levine and *I Have a Sister. My Sister Is Deaf* by Peterson, can be used to introduce necessary vocabulary, such as "deaf," "hearing impaired," "lip reading," "finger spelling," "sign language," and "soundless." Have the children try lip reading their names and familiar words. Have them consider the positions of the teeth, lips, tongue, etc., when they make various sounds.

b. After reading *Jamie's Tiger* by Wahl to the children, make a chart showing finger spelling and display it. Have each child learn to finger spell his/her own name. Let the children make up simple messages and transmit them through finger spelling. Charlip and Miller's nonfiction book *Handtalk* shows finger spelling of the alphabet through photographs. This book also illustrates some basic words and phrases in sign language that the children could practice.

c. Have the children dramatize various emotions by using nonverbal language such as facial expressions and bodily positions.

d. Nonfiction books such as Wolf's *Anna's Silent World* and Peter's *Claire and Emma* depict deaf children through photographs interacting with family and peers. Additional vocabulary that might be added from these books includes "audiologist," "hearing aid," and "decibel." As a follow-up activity to sharing these books, invite an expert to the classroom to show how hearing aids operate, how children wear them, and the like.

2) There are a number of books featuring a blind character that can serve as the springboard for activities.

a. *The Seeing Stick* by Yolen is a Chinese folk tale that emphasizes "seeing" through one's sense of touch. Collect a set of common objects that can be identified by touch and place them in a box. Blindfold individual children and have them identify the objects. In similar fashion, prepare swatches of material of varying textures, such as burlap, terry cloth, fur, velvet, satin, corduroy, etc., and have the children describe them while blindfolded. Prepare a set of sandpaper pictures on 4" x 6" index cards and have blindfolded children try to identify the pictured object. Start with simple pictures such as a circle, triangle, numerals, chair, table, rabbit, etc., and gradually use more complex outlines. Have the children make relief pictures using glue. After they have drawn a picture of an object, they outline it with two layers of white glue. After all the glue has dried completely, the outline of the object is raised from the surface of the paper. Blindfold the children and have them guess the pictures drawn by others in the class. Many of the above activities could be arranged in a learning center format to be done independently or with partners.

Older primary children, with adequate supervision, might carve pictures on balsa wood, thus making their own "seeing sticks" like the old man's in the story.

b. In *Through Grandpa's Eyes* by MacLachlan, the other senses take the place of sight. After sharing the book with the children, have them explore their sense of smell by identifying objects while blindfolded. Begin with objects that have strong, contrastive smells, such as an orange, peanut butter, an onion, etc.

Have the children become more aware of sound around them by engaging in quiet listening times. Keep records of the sounds heard while sitting quietly in the classroom and out on the playground or in the schoolyard. Have the children list sounds they hear at home in the morning before they get up or at night before they go to sleep. Compile their lists at school.

Play "Who Am I?" games. In one version, one child sits with his/her back to the group. Another child talks, and the first child tries to identify the talker by the sound of his/her voice. The game can also be played as a touching game. Blindfold some children and pair them with others. The blindfolded children touch the faces of their partners and try to guess whose face it is by feeling the features. Both of these games should be saved until the children know each other well.

In MacLachlan's book, the blind grandfather does exercises daily. Have the children do simple bending and stretching exercises while blindfolded. Make sure each child has lots of room to move, as orientation will be difficult.

c. Arrange the children in pairs, one blindfolded. Have the children walking as partners in the manner suggested in *The New Boy Is Blind* by Thomas. In this book, a boy learns the proper way to walk with his blind classmate.

d. Nonfiction books, such as *Connie's New Eyes* by Wolf and *Sally Can't See* by Peterson, can serve as the springboard for activities to help children become more knowledgeable about blindness. Secure some materials written in Braille for the children to examine. Make a chart of shapes used in Braille writing to represent letters and numbers. Have the children make code messages in Braille.

Have the children make a cassette tape and send it to a blind child at another school along with an invitation to return a tape in response. Taped correspondence can be maintained through the school year. This activity can be incorporated into a creative writing lesson, in which the children first write the messages that they want to put on the tape. They might also want to tape-record some of the stories that they have written and send them to their new friend.

Connie's New Eyes, explains the training of seeing eye dogs. If possible, have someone who trains guide dogs come into the classroom and talk to the children. Request that the speaker bring slides or pictures of dogs at various stages of their training.

Contact state and/or community agencies, such as the Society to Prevent Blindness and Rehabilitation Services for the Visually Impaired, to locate resource persons who will come and speak to the class.

3) Other physical handicaps are portrayed in children's books.

a. *A Look at Physical Handicaps* by Pursell can serve as an introduction of new vocabulary, including "paralyzed," "polio," "brace," "artificial limb," "prosthesis," "therapist," and the like. Other nonfiction books such as *Tracy* by Mack, *Janet at School* by White, and *Don't Feel Sorry for Paul* by Wold, use photographs to give information about the handicapping conditions as well as ways in which the children have adjusted. After sharing some of the books, invite a therapist who works with handicapped children to the classroom to speak.

b. After reading fictional stories such as Fassler's *Howie Helps Himself* and Lasker's *Nick Joins In*, obtain a wheelchair and give children an opportunity to try to maneuver it about the school building.

4) Informing children about the mentally handicapped is also a sensitive issue. It is hoped that sharing books with children will help them achieve a greater awareness and understanding of mentally handicapped persons. In many of the books featuring a mentally handicapped main character, that character is depicted as being "special" in terms of his/her own unique qualities and contributions. For example, in *Kelly's Creek* by Smith and *One Little Girl* by Fassler, the characters have special talents. As a follow-up activity to the reading of these books to the class, have children identify things that they do especially well. Use this discussion as an opportunity to promote self-worth and enhance the self-concept of each child. For this activity, children could write and illustrate stories about their special talents, hobbies, etc. This activity could also serve as an oral sharing time in which children bring in collections, photographs of themselves doing something special, and the like. Dealing with the critical level questions suggested earlier in this chapter can guide the discussion of books with mentally handicapped characters.

SELECTED BIBLIOGRAPHY OF BOOKS
ABOUT EXCEPTIONAL CHILDREN
PHYSICALLY HANDICAPPED

Bouchard, Lois Kalb. *The Boy Who Wouldn't Talk.* Il. by Ann Grifalconi. Doubleday, 1969. (blind — fiction)

Bourke, Lina. *Handmade ABC· A Manual Alphabet.* Addison-Wesley, 1981. (fingerspelling — nonfiction)

_____. *Signs of a Friend.* Addison-Wesley, 1982. (deaf — nonfiction)

Charlip, Remy and Mary Beth Miller. *Handtalk — An ABC of Finger Spelling and Sign Language.* Photographs by George Ancona. Parent's, 1974 (nonfiction)

Christopher, Matt. *Glue Fingers.* Il. by Jim Venable. Little, Brown, 1975. (stuttering — fiction)

Cohen, Miriam. *See You Tomorrow, Charles.* Il. by Lillian Hoban. Greenwillow, 1983. (blind — fiction)

Curtis, Patricia. *Cindy, A Hearing Ear Dog*. Photographs by David Cupp. Dutton, 1981. (nonfiction)

Fanshawe, Elizabeth. *Rachel*. Il. by Michael Charlton. Bradbury, 1975. (physical handicap — fiction)

Fassler, Joan. *Howie Helps Himself*. Il. by Joe Lasker. Whitman, 1975. (cerebral palsy — fiction)

Gold, Phyllis. *Please Don't Say Hello*. Human Sciences Press, 1975. (autism — fiction)

Greenfield, Eloise. *Darlene*. Il. by George Ford. Methuen, 1980. (physical handicap — fiction)

Griese, Arnold A. *At the Mouth of the Luckiest River*. Il. by Glo Coalson. Crowell, 1969. (physical handicap — fiction)

Heide, Florence Parry. *Sound of Sunshine, Sound of Rain*. Il. by Kenneth Longtemps. Parent's, 1970. (blind — fiction)

Keats, Ezra Jack. *Apt. 3*. Macmillan, 1971. (blind — fiction)

Lasker, Joe. *Nick Joins In*. Whitman, 1980. (physical handicap — fiction)

Levine, Edna S. *Lisa and Her Soundless World*. Il. by Gloria Kamen. Human Sciences Press, 1974. (deaf — nonfiction)

Litchfield, Ada B. *A Button in Her Ear*. Il. by Eleanor Mill. Whitman, 1976. (deaf — fiction)

_____. *A Cane in Her Hand*. Il. by Eleanor Mill. Whitman, 1977. (visually handicapped — fiction)

_____. *Captain Hook, That's Me*. Il. by Sonia Lisker. Walker, 1982. (physical handicap — fiction)

Mack, Nancy. *Tracy*. Photographs by Heinz Kluetmeier. Raintree, 1976. (cerebral palsy — nonfiction)

MacLachlan, Patricia. *Through Grandpa's Eyes*. Il. by Deborah Ray. Harper & Row, 1980. (blind — fiction)

Naylor, Phyllis. *Jennifer Jean, the Cross-Eyed Queen*. Il. by Harold Lamson. Lerner, 1967. (visually handicapped — fiction)

Peter, Diana. *Claire and Emma*. Photographs by Jeremy Finlay. John Day, 1976. (deaf — nonfiction)

Peterson, Jeanne Whitehouse. *I Have a Sister — My Sister is Deaf*. Il. by Deborah Ray. Harper & Row, 1977. (deaf — fiction)

Peterson, Palle. *Sally Can't See*. John Day, 1974. (blind — nonfiction)

Pursell, Margaret Sandford. *A Look at Physical Handicaps*. Photographs by Maria S. Forrai. Lerner, 1976. (general — nonfiction)

Rosenberg, Maxine B. *My Friend Leslie*. Photographs by George Ancona. Lothrop, 1983. (multiple handicaps — nonfiction)

Stanek, Muriel. *Growl When You Say R*. Il. by Phil Stein. Whitman, 1979. (speech impediment — fiction)

Stein, Sara Bonnett. *About Handicaps*. Photographs by Dick Frank. Walker, 1974. (physical handicap — nonfiction)

Thomas, William E. *The New Boy is Blind*. Messner, 1980. (blind — nonfiction)

Turnbull, Agnes Sligh. *The White Lark*. Il. by Nathan Goldstein. Houghton, 1968. (physical handicap — fiction)

Vance, Marguerite. *Windows for Rosemary*. Il. by Robert Doares. Dutton, 1956. (blind — fiction)

Wahl, Jan. *Jamie's Tiger*. Il. by Tomie de Paola. Harcourt, 1978. (deaf — fiction)

_____. *Button Eye's Orange*. Il. by Wendy Watson. Warne, 1980. (physical handicap — fiction)

White, Paul. *Janet at School*. Photographs by Jeremy Finlay. John Day, 1976. (physical handicap — nonfiction)

Wolf, Bernard. *Don't Feel Sorry for Paul*. Lippincott, 1974. (physical handicap — nonfiction)

_____. *Connie's New Eyes*. Lippincott, 1976. (blind — nonfiction)

_____. *Anna's Silent World*. Lippincott, 1977. (deaf — nonfiction)

Wosmek, Frances. *A Bowl of Sun*. Children's Press, 1976. (blind — fiction)

Yolen, Jane. *The Seeing Stick*. Il. by Remy Charlip and Demetra Maraslis. Crowell, 1977. (blind — fiction)

MENTALLY HANDICAPPED

Anders, Rebecca. *A Look at Mental Retardation*. Photographs by Maria S. Forrai. Lerner, 1976. (nonfiction)

Brightman, Alan. *Like Me*. Little, Brown, 1976. (nonfiction)

Clifton, Lucille. *My Friend Jacob*. Il. by Thomas Digrazia. Dutton, 1980.

Fassler, Joan. *One Little Girl*. Il. by M. Jane Smyth. Human Sciences Press, 1969. (fiction)

Hasler, Eveline. *Martin is Our Friend*. Il. by Dorothea Desmarowitz. Abingdon, 1981. (fiction)

Larsen, Hanne. *Don't Forget Tom*. Crowell, 1978. (nonfiction)

Lasker, Joe. *He's My Brother*. Whitman, 1974. (fiction)

Ominsky, Elaine. *Jon O., A Special Boy*. Il. by Dennis Simonetti. Prentice-Hall, 1977. (nonfiction)

Smith, Doris Buchanan. *Kelly's Creek*. Il. by Alan Tiegreen. Crowell, 1975. (fiction)

Smith, Lucia B. *A Special Kind of Sister*. Il. by Chuck Hall. Holt, 1979. (fiction)

Sobol, Harriet Langsam. *My Brother Steven is Retarded*. Photographs by Patricia Agre. Macmillan, 1977. (nonfiction)

CHAPTER SIX

Poetry

Young children have a natural appreciation for rhythmic language. In the primary grades, the emphasis in using poetry should be on reading poems aloud. Analysis of poetic form and meaning is not particularly important at this stage. Memorization of poems should not be required. Children will frequently learn favorite poems on their own simply because they like them. Poetry should also not be set aside as a specific unit of study. It should be integrated into classroom routine. There are truly poems for all occasions. Poems of all kinds should be shared with children — often! Beatrice Shenk deRegniers in *Poems Children Will Sit Still For* offers these hints for reading poetry to children:

Read only poems that you, the teacher, like.

Read the poem aloud before reading it to the children.

Read slowly enough so that the children can understand the ideas presented.

Read in a natural tone of voice with whatever expression is appropriate.

Enjoy the reading of poetry, and the children will share in the enjoyment.

The reading of poetry does not *require* follow-up activities. Any such activities, however, should enhance the appreciation of the poems. The ideas suggested in this chapter are of a general nature that can be applied to a variety of poems. Activities for specific poems and collections of poems, however, are also presented.

Writing Poetry

Poetry writing in the primary grades should be done on a limited basis. It is best left to small and/or large group composition. Rhyme and meter should not be points of emphasis. Greater success in writing is assured when the topics are very familiar to the children.

MY DOG	OREOS
Sunshine has a freckly nose.	Oreo cookies are black and white.
Everywhere I go, she goes.	First I lick the icing, then I bite!

Two forms of unrhymed poetry may be introduced in the primary grades: cinquain (sin-kane) and concrete poetry. One form of a cinquain is a five line poem with the following format:

Line 1 — one word, giving the title

Line 2 — two words, describing the title

Line 3 — three words, expressing action (participles)

Line 4 — four words, expressing a feeling/giving information

Line 5 — one word, another word for the title

Children should have plenty of experience writing cinquains in groups before attempting to write their own.

Kitten	Apple
Fluffy, cuddly	Crunchy, juicy
Bouncing, napping, purring	Picking, peeling, eating
Sometimes scratches my face	Keeps the doctor away
Tiger.	Delicious.

Concrete poetry is visual poetry. The letters, words, and sentences form a picture.

jumps   road   in the

A grasshopper   across the   to hide   grass.

Two books by Robert Froman, *Street Poems* and *Seeing Things*, give many examples of concrete poetry.

Dramatization Activities

Many poems lend themselves well to pantomime and creative dramatization. Children may try out the various ways of walking described in these poems:

ON OUR WAY

What kind of walk shall we take today?
Leap like a frog? Creep like a snail?
Scamper like a squirrel with a furry tail?

Flutter like a butterfly? Chicken peck?
Stretch like a turtle with a poking-out neck?

Trot like a pony, clip clop clop?
Swing like a monkey in a treetop?

Scuttle like a crab? Kangaroo jump?
Plod like a camel with an up-and-down hump?

We could even try a brand new way —
Walking down the street
On our own two feet.

     by Eve Merriam (*Catch A Little Rhyme*)

JUMP OR JIGGLE

Frogs jump
Caterpillars hump

Worms wiggle
Bugs jiggle

Rabbits hop
Horses clop

Snakes slide
Seagulls glide

Mice creep
Deer leap

Puppies bounce
Kittens pounce

Lions stalk —
But —
I walk!

     by Evelyn Beyer (*Time for Poetry*)

Children may pantomime some of the actions suggested below after hearing this poem from *Near the Window Tree* by Karla Kushkin:

Buggity
Buggity
Bug
Wandering aimlessly
Buggishly smug
When all of a sudden along came a shoe
Out with another shoe
Wandering too.
The shoes went on wandering:
Left,
Right,
Left,
Splat.

Bugs
Very frequently perish like that.
Pantomimes:

different kinds of bugs walking
a bug walking, oblivious to danger
two BIG shoes, walking heavily
shoes marching left, right, left, . . .
stepping on a bug

The following poem by Valerie Worth from *Still More Small Poems* is appropriate for pantomime:

Barefoot

After that tight
Choke of sock
And blunt
Weight of shoe,

The foot can feel
Clover's green
Skin
Growing,

And the fine
Invisible
Teeth
Of gentle grass,

And the cool
Breath
Of the earth
Beneath.

Pantomimes:

walking in uncomfortable shoes
lifting foot wearing *very* heavy shoe
taking off a heavy shoe (untying big laces,
etc.)
taking off a thick sock
wriggling toes in relief
running barefoot in the grass

Teachers will want to develop pantomime activities from other poems that the children like. Children may want to suggest pantomimes of their own for poems. Children might use rhythm instruments and sound effects to accompany this poem:

THE MARCHING BAND

I'd like to be in the marching band
And step high with my feet
Left — Right — Left — Right,
Keeping time with the drummer's beat.

What should I play in the marching band?
Cymbals (CRASH!)? or horn (taaah-taaah!)?
Drum (rum-pum!)? or bell (ting-ting!)?
Or a giant tuba (oom-pah-pah-pah!)?

I'd like to be in the marching band
With the bright flags flying high,
While crowds of people along the street
Clap as we proudly march by.

Children could dramatize by marching, playing instruments, tossing a baton, cheering, clapping, and waving.

"The Little Turtle" by Vachel Lindsay can be adapted to a circle game.

THE LITTLE TURTLE

There was a little turtle.
He lived in a box.
He swam in a puddle.
He climbed on the rocks.

He snapped at a mosquito.
He snapped at a flea.
He snapped at a minnow.
And he snapped at me.

He caught the mosquito.
He caught the flea.
He caught the minnow.
But he didn't catch me.

A gym floor is the best place for this game because a fixed circle, such as one painted on the floor, is needed. One child is the "turtle" and stands in the center of the circle. The other children are randomly scattered within the bounds of the circle. The children recite the first and second verses as they walk around within the circle. When they say "me," the "turtle" attempts to catch as many children as possible. Caution the children that they must stay within the circle during the tagging. Allow the "turtle" to tag for 4-5 seconds and blow a whistle to stop. Children who are tagged must leave the circle. Proceed with the last verse. Select a different "turtle" for each game.

Sharing Poetry

To motivate the sharing of poetry with the children, designate one bulletin board in the classroom for poetry. Change the theme of the bulletin board each month according to seasons, holidays, and special days. Display a number of poems in keeping with the theme. Let the children choose a poem from the board for the teacher to read periodically. Several of the poems may be read more than once as the children choose those that they want to hear.

Suggestions and patterns for poetry bulletin boards from September through May are included here.

SEPTEMBER

Poems having to do with autumn, leaves turning, harvest time. school starting, etc., are needed. Put a poem on each leaf. Put as many leaves as desired on the tree.

OCTOBER

Put a Halloween poem on each gravestone. Put as many gravestones as desired on the bulletin board.

NOVEMBER

Make construction paper feathers of different colors. Put a Thanksgiving poem on each feather. Put as many feathers on the turkey as desired.

DECEMBER

Cut ornaments of different colored construction paper. Put a Christmas poem on each. Make ornaments in different shapes if desired. The ornaments may be decorated with glitter.

111

JANUARY

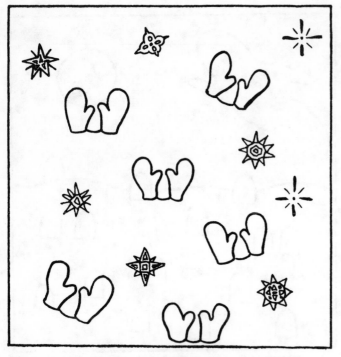

Cut out paper snowflakes to put on a blue background. Cut out construction paper mittens in different colors. Join mittens together with yarn.

FEBRUARY

Make hearts from pink, red, or white paper. Decorate with paper doilies, etc. Use Lincoln, Washington, and Groundhog's Day poems also.

MARCH

Cut kites from different colored construction paper. Attach yarn for tails. Use poems about wind, kite flying, St. Patrick's Day, etc., and Easter, if in March.

APRIL

Make umbrellas from different colored construction paper. Make raindrops from waxed paper. Use poems about rain, spring, puddles, etc., and Easter, if in April.

MAY

Make flowers from pastel colored construction paper. Use poems about spring, flowers, warm weather, birds, green grass, etc.

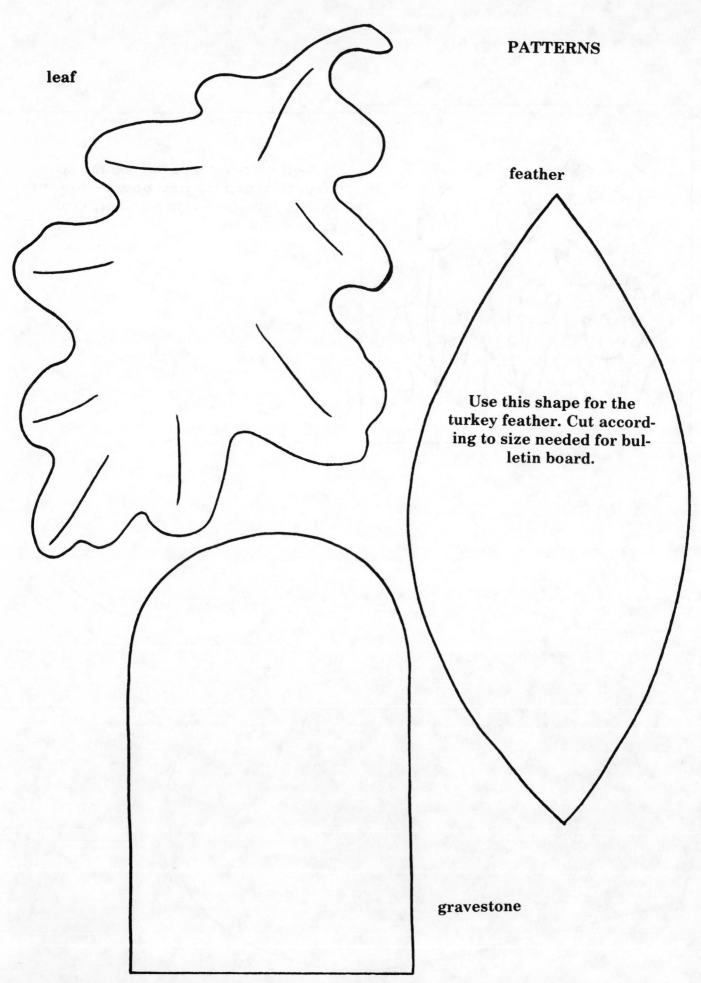

PATTERNS

leaf

feather

Use this shape for the
turkey feather. Cut according to size needed for bulletin board.

gravestone

114

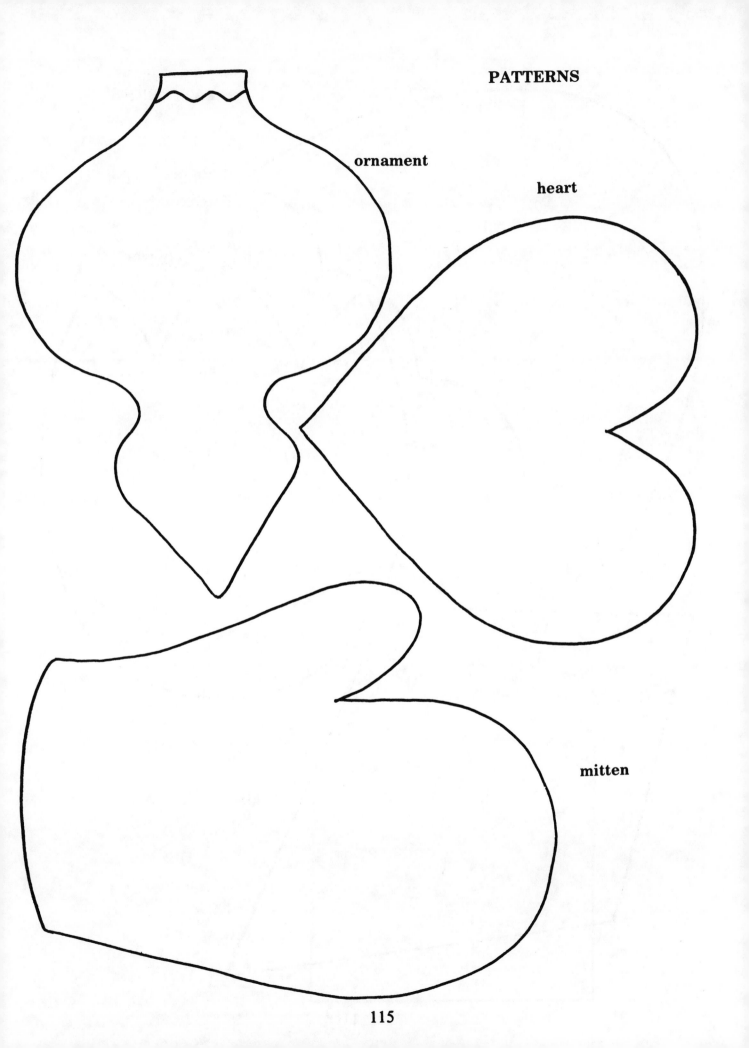

PATTERNS

ornament

heart

mitten

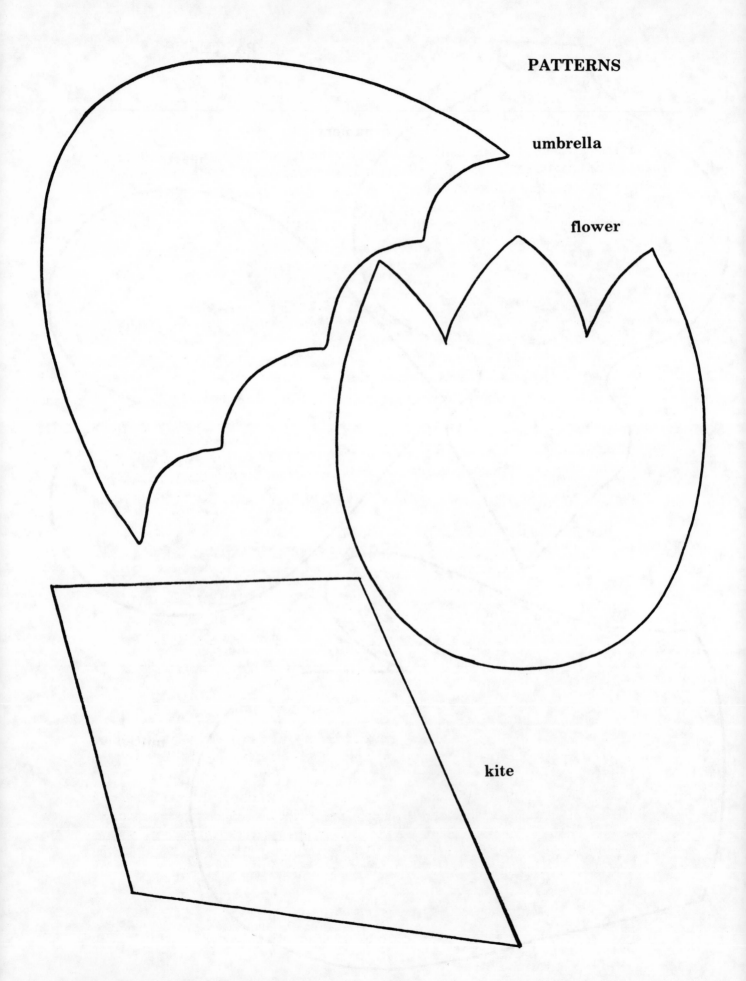

PATTERNS

umbrella

flower

kite

POETRY ACTIVITIES

1) Young children enjoy dogs and cats, and collections abound with poems about them. Make bulletin boards with pictures of dogs/cats (calendars are a good source), photos of the children's pet dogs/cats, or picturs of "wish" dogs/cats that the children have drawn. Have books of animal poems available. Children can locate poems that seem to describe their dogs and cats. Start a notebook of these poems. These books will be helpful:

Shaggy Dogs & Spotty Dogs & Shaggy & Spotty Dogs by Seymour Leichman
My Cat Has Eyes of Sapphire Blue. By Aileen Fisher
Feathered Ones and Furry by Aileen Fisher
The Cat Book by Richard Shaw
Hark! Hark! The Dogs Do Bark and Other Rhymes about Dogs by Lenore Blevgad
Mitten for Kittens: And Other Rhymes about Cats by Lenore Blevgad
Near the Window Tree by Karla Kushkin (cats)

2) Everyone has a favorite food. Have the children find pictures of different foods and poems to go with the pictures. Use the books, *How to Eat a Poem and Other Morsels* by Rose Agree and *Eats* by Arnold Adoff, to get them started. Let them make a bulletin board of their favorites. (There is even a poem about pizza in Ogden Nash's *Custard and Company*.) They also might like to write some cinquain poetry about foods and compile them in shape books like these:

Cut writing paper in the shape of the book. Have the children write their cinquain poems. Bind with loose leaf rings between construction paper covers. Display the "books" with the bulletin board.

3) Using *Some of the Days of Everett Anderson* by Lucille Clifton as a stimulus, generate a discussion of what children like to do on different days of the week. Using the sentence patterns from the book, have the children work in small groups and dictate their "days" poems. Use names of different children in place of "Everett Anderson" in the poems. Compile the poems of each group into books, titled "Some of the Days of the . . . Group."

4) Young children love to make sounds. After sharing *Who, Said Sue, Said Whoo?* by Ellen Raskin with them, have the children make a mural of all the animals pictured in the book. They can add trees to help camouflage some of them. Label the animal sounds. Share other books that focus on sounds, such as these:

Roar and More by Karla Kuskin
Out Loud by Eve Merriam
Listen! Listen! by Ann Rand

After children have heard some of the poems in these books, they may want to join in on the sounds.

5) To develop color concepts, Mary O'Neill's *Hailstones and Halibut Bones* and Christina Rossetti's *What Is Pink?* will be helpful. Share the poems with the children over a period of several days. Have them make color charts by cutting out pictures of objects of various colors. Following simple patterns, they can write descriptive sentences for their chart, such as, "Red is a rose, a tomato is red." Children may even suggest a rhyming pattern, such as "Red is a rose, and when it's cold, so is your nose."

6) Using *All My Shoes Come In Twos* by Mary Ann and Norman Hoberman as a stimulus, set up a table display of pairs of shoes. Have the children help collect as many different kinds of shoes as possible. Put copies of the poems from the book in the appropriate shoes. Have the children see if they can locate other poems about shoes to put in the shoes. Have some paper bare feet on the table also for poems about going barefoot. After the children have read and heard several of the poems, try writing a class poem in which individual children contribute a line about a favorite pair of shoes.

7) Using the pattern of Edward Lear's "Nonsense Alphabet," the children could write their own alphabet rhymes and illustrate them. In Lear's alphabet:

H was once a little hen,
　　Henny
　　Chenny
　　Tenny
　　Henny
　Eggsy-any
Little Hen?

The children might come up with the following:

H was once a little horse,
　　Horsy
　　Norsy
　　Gorsy
　　Horsy
　Ride, of coursey,
Little Horse.

8) Share *Nuts to You and Nuts to Me: An Alphabet of Poems* by Mary Ann Hoberman with the children. Have them develop lists of words that begin with the same sound. Let them think of ways to string the words together to make short alliterative poems like those in the book.

9) Share the poems in the book *Do Bears Have Mothers Too?* by Aileen Fisher over a period of days. The two activities suggested below, matching animal names with names of their offspring, can be done independently by the children. For this activity, you will need a cardboard pizza round and some clothespins. Divide the circle into sections. Glue or draw pictures of animals around the center of the circle. Around the edge of the circle, put a red dot and a blue dot in each section. Code the clothespins with either a red dot *or* a blue dot. On the clothespins marked with a red dot, put the name of the animal baby. On the pins with blue dots, put the adult name. Give these directions to the children: Clip the red dot pins to the red dots on the circle and the blue dot pins to the blue dots on the circle, matching the animal words to the picture. For self-checking, code the back of the circle with the correct words.

The puzzle activity shown below can be made from laminated poster board. Pieces fit together for self-checking.

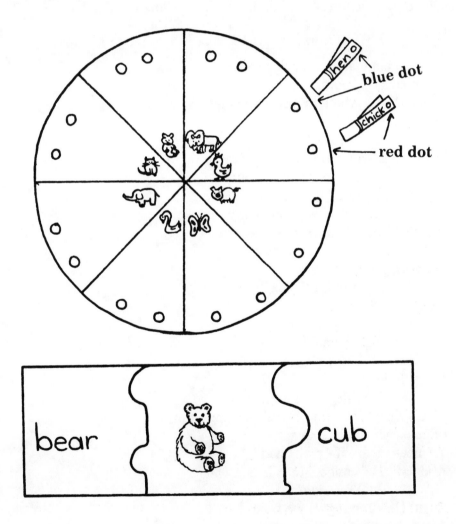

Suggested adult-baby animal pairs:

bear - cub	fox - pup	butterfly - caterpillar
deer - fawn	swan - cygnet	frog - tadpole
dog - puppy	horse - colt	pig - piglet
cat - kitten	hen - chick	kangaroo - joey
cow - calf	penguin - chick	sheep - lamb
elephant - calf	goose - gosling	lion - cub
giraffe - calf	duck - duckling	goat - kid

10) Children enjoy riddles and games. Many of the poems in John Ciardi's *I Met a Man* are riddle-type poems that supply clues through rhyme and invite the children to guess what "man" each poem is describing. The poem "I Met a Man That Was Playing Games" is a rhyming word game to which the children could add many more lines.

I MET A MAN THAT WAS PLAYING GAMES

I met a man that was playing games.
What kind of games?
        About things and names.
How do you play?
        He didn't say.
But from what I heard, it goes this way:
I pick a rhyme — let's say it's "any"
If I say "Spend it," you say *penny*.
If I say "Girl," then you say *Jenny*.
If I say "Boy," then you say *Kenny*.
Yes, I see. May I pick one now?
What do you pick?
        Well, I'll pick "how"
And I say "Milk it."
        I say *cow*.
I say "It's right here."
        Then it's *now*.
I say "It hurts."
        Ouch!. . . I mean *Ow!*
That's right. You turn now. This game's fun.
I'll make it fast, for I have to run
To meet a man. If I pick "had"
And say "He's mine," than he's . . .
        Your *dad!*
Right! He's coming on the train.
After supper let's play again!

11) Children are fascinated with monsters. Daisy Wallace's collection, *Monster Poems*, contains numerous poems that can serve as the basis for creative activities. "The

Monster Pet" by Lilian Moore can be the focal point of a display of drawings by the children of "pets" that a monster might have. "Monster Menu" by Florence Parry Heide might stimulate children to write menus to serve when they invite a monster for lunch. Children could add lines describing places where monsters might lurk to Steven Kroll's poem "Monsters Everywhere." They could also make a mural of this poem. The last poem in the book, "In a Dark Wood" can be adapted to choral reading by the children.

12) Not only will children enjoy chiming in on the repetitive phrases of Maurice Sendak's *Chicken Soup With Rice*, but they might also compose group poems of what they like to do during each month of the year. These poems should be compiled into a book of "months" poems.

SELECTED BIBLIOGRAPHY OF POETRY BOOKS

Adoff, Arnold. *Eats. Poems*. Il. by Susan Russo. Othrop, 1979.

_____. *Sister Tells Me That I'm Black*. Il. by Lorenzo Lynch. Holt, 1976.

Agree, Rose (com.). *How to Eat a Poem and Other Morsels*. Il. by Peggy Wilson. Pantheon, 1967.

Aldis, Dorothy. *The Secret Place and Other Poems*. Il. by Olivia H. Cole. Putnam, 1962.

_____. *Is Anybody Hungry?* Il. by Artur Marokvia. Putnam, 1964.

Asch, Frank. *Country Pie*. Greenwillow, 1979.

Belloc, Hilaire. *The Yak, the Python, the Frog*. Parent's, 1975.

Bennett, Jill (comp.). *Roger Was a Razor Fish; and Other Poems*. Il. by Maureen Roffey. Lothrop, 1981.

_____. *Days are Where We Live*. Il. by Maureen Roffey. Lothrop, 1982.

_____. *Tiny Tim*. Il by Helen Oxenbury. Delacorte, 1982.

Blevgad, Lenore. *Hark! Hark! The Dogs Do Bark and Other Rhymes About Dogs*. Il. by Erik Blevgad. Atheneum, 1976.

_____. *Mittens For Kittens: and Other Rhymes About Cats*. Il. by Erik Blevgad. Atheneum, 1974.

_____. *The Parrot in the Garret and Other Rhymes About Dwellings*. Il. by Erik Blevgad. Atheneum, 1982.

Bodecker, N.M. *Let's Marry, Said the Cherry*. Atheneum, 1974.

_____. *Snowman Sniffles*. Atheneum, 1983.

Brooks, Gwendolyn. *Bronzeville Boys and Girls*. Il. by Ronni Solbert. Harper & Row, 1956.

Brown, Margaret Wise. *Nibble, Nibble*. Il. by Leonard Weisgard. Scott, 1944.

Calmenson, Stephanie (sel.). *Never Take a Pig to Lunch*. Il. by Hilary Knight. Doubleday, 1982.

Chute, Marchette. *Rhymes About Us*. Dutton, 1974.

Ciardi, John. *I Met a Man*. Il. by Robert Osborn. Houghton, 1961.

_____. *Someone Could Win a Polar Bear*. Il. by Edward Gorey. Lippincott,

1970.

Clifton, Lucille. *Some of the Days of Everett Anderson*. Il. by Evaline Ness. Holt, 1970.

Cole, William (comp.). *I Went to the Animal Fair*. Il. by Colette Rosselli. World, 1958.

_____. *What's Good For a Six Year Old?* Il. by Ingrid Fetz. Holt, 1965.

_____. *What's Good For a Four Year Old?* Il. by Tomi Ungerer. Holt, 1967.

_____. *What's Good For a Five Year Old?* Il. by Edward Sorel. Holt, 1971.

_____. *What's Good For a Three Year Old?* Il. by Lillian Hoban. Holt, 1974.

_____. *An Arkful of Animals*. Il. by Lynn Munsinger. Houghton, 1978.

_____. *Good Dog Poems*. Il. by Ruth Sanderson. Scribner, 1981.

_____. *Poem Stew*. Il. by Karen Ann Weinhaus. Lippincott, 1981.

Craig, Jean (comp.). *The Sand, The Sea, and Me*. Il. by Audrey Newell. Walker, 1972.

de Regniers, Beatrice Schenk, et. al. *Poems Children Will Sit Still For*. Citation, 1969.

_____. *A Bunch of Poems and Verses*. Il. by Mary Jane Dunton. Seabury, 1977.

Field, Eugene. *Wynken, Blynken and Nod*. Il. by Susan Jeffers. Dutton, 1982.

Fisher, Aileen. *Cricket in a Thicket*. Il. by Feodor Rojankovsky. Scribner, 1963.

_____. *Feathered Ones and Furry*. Il. by Eric Carle. Crowell, 1971.

_____. *My Cat Has Eyes of Sapphire Blue*. Il. by Marie Angel. Crowell, 1973.

_____. *Do Bears Have Mothers Too?* Il. by Eric Carle. Crowell, 1971.

_____. *Out in the Dark and Daylight*. Il. by Gail Owens. Harper & Row, 1980.

_____. *Anybody Home?* Il. by Susan Bonners. Crowell, 1980.

Froman, Robert. *Street Poems*. McCall, 1971.

_____. *Seeing Things*. Crowell, 1974.

Frost, Robert. *Stopping by the Woods on a Snowy Evening*. Il. by Susan Jeffers. Dutton, 1978.

Greenfield, Eloise. *Honey, I Love*. Il. by Leo and Diane Dillon. Crowell, 1978.

Haley, Gail. *One, Two, Buckle My Shoe*. Doubleday, 1964.

Hoban, Russell. *Egg Thought and Other Frances Songs*. Il. by Lillian Hoban. Harper & Row, 1972.

Hoberman, Mary Ann. *A Little Book of Beasts*. Il. by Peter Parnall. Simon & Schuster, 1973.

_____. *Nuts to You and Nuts to Me: An Alphabet of Poems*. Il. by Ronni Solbert. Knopf, 1974.

_____. *Bugs*. Il. by Victoria Chess. Viking, 1976.

_____. *Yellow Butter Purple Jelly Red Jam Black Bread*. Il. by Chaya Burstein. Viking, 1981.

_____. *The Cozy Book*. Il. by Tony Chen. Viking, 1982.

Hoberman, Mary Ann and Norman Hoberman. *All My Shoes Come in Twos*. Little, Brown, 1957.

Hopkins, Lee Bennett (comp.). *Me! A Book of Poems*. Seabury, 1970.

_____. *Girls Can Too*. Il. by Emily Arnold McCully. Watts, 1972.

_____. *Hey-How for Halloween*. Il. by Janet McCaffery. Harcourt, 1974.

_____. *Sing Hey for Christmas Day*. Il. by Laura Jean Allen. Harcourt, 1975.

_____. *Good Morning to You, Valentine*. Il. by Tomie de Paola. Harcourt, 1976.

_____. *A-Haunting We Will Go*. Whitman, 1977.

_____. *Beat the Drum: Independence Day Has Come*. Il. by Tomie de Paola. Harcourt, 1977.

_____. *Merrily Comes Our Harvest In*. Il. by Ben Schecter. Harcourt, 1978.

_____. *Easter Buds are Springing*. Il. by Tomie de Paola. Harcourt, 1979.

_____. *Go to Bed! A Book of Bedtime Poems*. Il. by Rosekrans Hoffman. Knopf, 1979.

_____. *Elves, Fairies, and Gnomes*. Il. by Rosekrans Hoffman. Knopf, 1980.

_____. *Circus! Circus!* Il. by John O'Brien. Knopf, 1982.

Kuskin, Karla. *Roar and More*. Harper & Row, 1956.

_____. *Near the Window Tree*. Harper & Row, 1975.

Lee, Dennis. *Nicholas Knock and Other People*. Il. by Frank Newfeld. Houghton, 1974.

_____. *Alligator Pie*. Il. by Frank Newfeld. Houghton, 1975.

Leichman, Seymour. *Shaggy Dogs & Spotty Dogs & Shaggy & Spotty Dogs*. Harcourt, 1973.

Lenski, Lois. *City Poems*. Walck, 1971.

Livingston, Myra Cohn. *Whispers and Other Poems*. Harcourt, 1959.

_____. *Wide Awake and Other Poems*. Harcourt, 1959.

_____. (ed.). *O Frabjous Day! Poetry for Holidays and Special Occasions*. Atheneum, 1977.

Marzollo, Jean. *Close Your Eyes*. Il. by Susan Jeffers. Dial, 1978.

McCord, David. *Every Time I Climb a Tree*. Il. by Marc Simont. Little, Brown, 1967.

_____. *The Star in the Pail*. Il. by Marc Simont. Little, Brown, 1975.

Merriam, Eve. *Catch a Little Rhyme*. Atheneum, 1966.

_____. *Out Loud*. Atheneum, 1973.

Milne, A.A. *Now We Are Six*. Il. by E.H. Shepard. Dutton, 1927.

Moore, Lillian. *Spooky Rhymes and Riddles*. Il. by Ib Ohlsson. Scholastic, 1972.

_____. *See My Lovely Poison Ivy and Other Verses About Witches, Ghosts, and Things*. Il. by Diane Dawson. Atheneum, 1975.

Nash, Ogden. *Custard and Company*. Sel. and Il. by Quentin Blake. Little, Brown, 1980.

Ness, Evaline. *Amelia Mixed the Mustard and Other Poems*. Scribner, 1975.

O'Neill, Mary. *Hailstones and Halibut Bones*. Il. by Leonard Weisgard. Doubleday, 1961.

Pomerantz, Charlotte. *The Tamarindo Puppy; and Other Poems*. Il. by Byron Barton. Greenwillow, 1980.

Prelutsky, Jack. *A Gopher in the Garden and Other Animal Poems*. Il. by Robert Leydenfrost .Macmillan, 1967.

_____. *Toucans Two and Other Poems*. Il. by Jose Aruego. Macmillan, 1970.

_____. *The Queen of Eene*. Il. by Victoria Chess. Greenwillow, 1978.

_____. *Rolling Harvey Down the Hill*. Il. by Victoria Chess. Greenwillow, 1980.

_____. *Rainy Rainy Saturday*. Il. by Marilyn Hafner. Greenwillow, 1980.

_____. *The Sheriff of Rottenshot*. Il. by Victoria Chess. Greenwillow, 1982.

Rand, Ann. *Listen! Listen!* Il. by Paul Rand. Harcourt, 1970.

Raskin, Ellen. *Silly Songs and Sad*. Crowell, 1967.

_____. *Who, Said Sue, Said Whoo?*. Atheneum, 1973.

Riley, James Whitcomb. *The Gobble-Uns'll Git You Ef You Don't Watch Out!* Il. by Joel Schick. Lippincott, 1975.

Rosen, Michael. *You Can't Catch Me*. Il. by Quentin Blake. Dutton, 1982.

Rossetti Christina. *What is Pink?* Il. by Jose Aruego. Macmillan, 1971.

Sendak, Maurice. *Chicken Soup With Rice*. Harper & Row, 1962.

Schick, Eleanor. *City Green* .Macmillan, 1974.

Shaw, Richard (ed.). *The Cat Book*. Warne, 1973.

_____. *The Mouse Book* .Warne, 1975.

Siverstein, Shel. *Where the Sidewalk Ends*. Harper & Row, 1974.

Thurman, Judith. *Flashlight*. Il. by Reina Rubel. Atheneum, 1976.

Tippett, James, *Crickety-Cricket! The Best Loved Poems of James S. Tippett*. Harper & Row, 1973.

Tripp, Wallace. *A Great Big Ugly Man Came Up and Tied His Horse to Me*. Little, Brown, 1973.

Wallace, Daisy (ed.). *Witch Poems*. Il. by Trina Schart Hyman. Holiday, 1976.

_____. *Monster Poems*. Il. by Kay Chorao. Holiday, 1976.

_____. *Ghost Poems*. Il. by Tomie de Paola. Holiday, 1979.

_____. *Fairy Poems*. Il. by Trina Schart Hyman. Holiday, 1980.

Watson, Clyde. *Father Fox's Pennyrhymes*. Il. by Wendy Watson. Crowell, 1971.

Worth, Valerie. *Small Poems*. Il. by Natalie Babbitt. Farrar, 1972.

_____. *More Small Poems*. Il. by Natalie Babbitt. Farrar, 1976.

_____. *Still More Small Poems*. Il. by Natalie Babbitt. Farrar, 1978.

CHAPTER SEVEN

Concept and Informational Books

Concept Books

BASIC CONCEPTS

Concepts are best developed through active participation by the children with manipulatives and by dramatization. Concept books enhance language development and help children expand and refine basic concepts. There are several books which can serve as a stimulus for oral discussion as well as a springboard for group activities. A bibliography of books dealing with a variety of concepts is included at the end of this section.

1) Have the children make a large mural based on Poulet's *Blue Bug's Vegetable Garden*. They can make vegetables that grow *under* the ground, such as radishes, beets, carrots, potatoes, and turnips, and those that grow *above* the ground. Children can also make comparisons between *tall* vegetables, such as corn, and those the grow relatively *short* and close to the ground, such as lettuce. The book makes use of many positional words which could be used for labeling the mural.

2) Read the book *Rosie's Walk* by Hutchins. Have the children pantomime Rosie and the fox. Emphasize positional words while they dramatize:

> The fox is sneaking *behind* Rosie.
> Rosie is walking *under* the beehives.
> Rosie is walking *around* the pond.
> Rosie is walking *over* the haystack.
> The fox fell *into* the haystack.
>
> Tables and chairs in the room can serve as the props needed for the dramatizations (the haystack, beehives, the mill, etc.). An animated film of "Rosie's Walk" is also available from Weston Woods, Inc.

3) Games and relays are helpful for the development of positional concepts. Games such as "London Bridge Is Falling Down" and "Squirrels and Trees" involve children in walking *under, between, inside,* etc., while hands go *up* and *down*. Ball-passing relays reinforce concepts of *over* and *under, between* the legs, and running *around* the *front* or *back* of the line, and the like.

4) Relational concepts can be reinforced using a magnetic board and Wells' *Max's Ride* as a stimulus. (A simple and inexpensive magnetic board can be made from an old cookie sheet with sides. Construction paper background scenes can be put in and taken out as needed. Individual pieces with a small piece of magnetic tape stuck to the back will adhere to the background. Magnetic tape can be purchased at hardware stores and crafts shops.) For this particular activity, the background scene need only have a few simple objects, such as a tree, a fence, a wagon, a basket, a few flowers, etc., as shown:

Where can Max go?

Max

Give the children directions such as these for placing Max on the board:

      under the tree
      on the fence
      in the basket
      above the wagon
      between the flowers
      beside the basket
      near the tree

Add others to develop additional concepts. This could be made into an independent activity by putting these directions on a cassette tape.

5) After sharing Banchek's *Snake In, Snake Out* with the children, have them do the snake sewing card as shown at the end of this section. Sewing reinforces over and under, in and out, up and down motions. The book is wordless except for the one-word labels, *in, out, under, on, off, over, up, down* on the pages. The illustrations offer opportunities for oral discussion.

6) *Left and Right With Lion and Ryan* by Littell uses a questioning format which invites the children to respond whether Lion is on the right side or left side in various situations. After sharing the book with the children, the activity may be carried on further by using a stuffed animal lion and providing left and right situations for it in the classroom. For example:

Put Lion on the right side of the block.
Is Lion on the right side or the left side of the book?
Put Lion on the left side of the box.

Children might want to make up their own left-right directions/questions for other to do/answer.

7) The photographs in Hoban's books, *Push-Pull, Empty-Full* and *Over, Under and Through*, offer opportunities for simple dramatization activities and oral discussion.

8) Have the children work in small groups to develop a book with a story and pictures patterned after Carle's *The Secret Birthday Message*. As a language experience activity, the children dictate the directions for finding the surprise present. Then they make a picture to go with each direction. The illustrations in the Carle book are die-cut, and the children could make their pictures in similar fashion (a pointed page for a mountain, for example). The directions and pictures could be put into a book which could be shared with other members of the class or other classes. Besides relational concepts, *The Secret Birthday Message* develops simple map-making skills and gives practice in following directions.

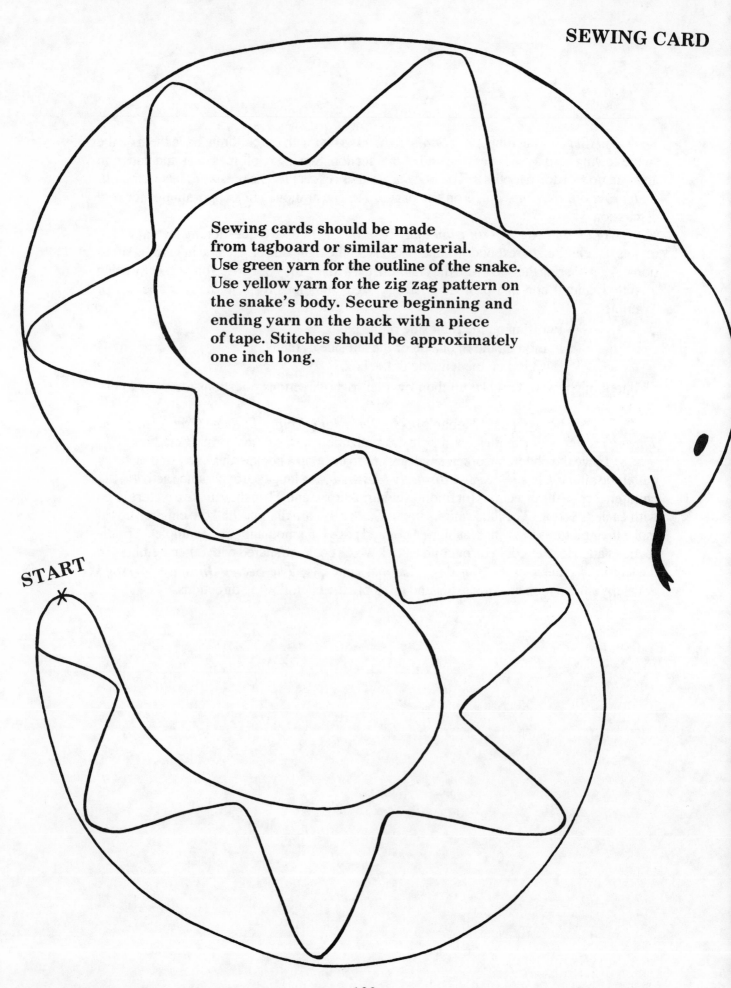

SEWING CARD

Sewing cards should be made
from tagboard or similar material.
Use green yarn for the outline of the snake.
Use yellow yarn for the zig zag pattern on
the snake's body. Secure beginning and
ending yarn on the back with a piece
of tape. Stitches should be approximately
one inch long.

START

9) Bester's *Guess What?* uses few words and photographs of animals and offers excellent preparation for the comprehension skill of making predictions as well as for basic concept development.

10) *The Very Hungry Caterpillar* by Carle is easily adapted to the flannel board. After children have heard the story and seen a demonstration by the teacher, they could work in pairs telling the story to each other. Have a copy of the book available at the flannel board for the children to use if needed.

SELECTED BIBLIOGRAPHY OF CONCEPT BOOKS

Banchek, Linda. *Snake In, Snake Out*. Il. by Elaine Arnold. Crowell, 1978.
Barton, Byron. *Wheels*. Crowell, 1979.
_____. *Building a House*. Greenwillow, 1981.
_____. *Airport*. Crowell, 1982.
Bester, Roger. *Guess What?* Crown, 1980.
_____. *Fireman Jim*. Crown, 1981.
Carle, Eric. *The Secret Birthday Message*. Crowell, 1971.
_____. *The Grouchy Lady Bug*. Crowell, 1977.
_____. *The Very Hungry Caterpillar*. World, 1969.
Crew, Donald. *Harbor*. Greenwillow, 1982.
Demi. *Where Is It?* Doubleday, 1979.
Gibbons, Gail. *The Post Office Book*. Crowell, 1982.
_____. *Tool Book*. Holiday, 1982.
Goor, Ron. *Shadows· Here, There and Everywhere*. Il. by Ron and Nancy Goor. Crowell, 1981.
Hoban, Tana. *Push-Pull, Empty-Full*. Macmillan, 1972.
_____. *Over Under and Through*. Macmillan, 1973.
_____. *Dig, Drill, Dump, Fill*. Greenwillow, 1975.
Hutchings, Pat. *Rosie's Walk*. Macmillan, 1968.
Littell, Robert. *Left and Right with Lion and Ryan*. Il. by Philip Wende. Cowles Book Company, 1969.
Maestro, Betsy. *Harriet Reads Signs and More Signs*. Il. by Betsy and Giulio Maestro. Crown, 1981.
_____. *Traffic· A Book of Opposites*. Il. by Guilio Maestro. Crown, 1981.
McMillan, Bruce. *Here a Chick, There a Chick*. Lothrop, 1983.
Martin, Bill, Jr. *Little Princess Good Night*. Il. by Joseph Domjan. Holt, 1967.
McNaughton, Colin. Opposites series (*At the Park, At the Playschool, At the Party, At Home* and *At the Store*). Philomel, 1982.
Opposites. (Series). Grosset and Dunlap.

Spier, Peter. *Fast-Slow, High-Low*. Doubleday, 1972.

_____. "Village Books" (*Bill's Service Station, The Firehouse, The Food Market, My School, The Pet Store, The Toy Shop*). Doubleday, 1982.

Tafuri, Nancy. *All Year Long*. Greenwillow, 1982.

Testa, Fulvio. *If You Take a Paintbrush*. Dial, 1983.

Wells, Rosemary. *Max's Ride*. Dial, 1979.

Wildsmith, Brian. *What the Moon Saw*. Oxford, 1978.

_____. *Big and Little*.

_____. *Front and Back*.

_____. *Top and Bottom*.

_____. *Old and New*.

_____. *Fast and Slow*.

_____. *Noisy and Quiet*.

Poulet, Virginia. *Blue Bug's Vegetable Garden*. Children's Press, 1973.

Rockwell, Anne. *Boats*. Dutton, 1982.

Solomon, Hannah. *Mouse Days· A Book of Seasons*. Il. by Leo Lionni. Pantheon, 1981.

COLOR CENTER

Note: Since the children participating in the activities of this center may not be reading as yet, the teacher will need to read the recommended books to the children prior to doing the activities.

The color center is introduced to the children by the book *Green Says Go* by Ed Emberley. A large stoplight suspended from the ceiling provides the overall organization of this three-part center.

1) The first part is "GO on a Freight Train Ride" based on the book *Freight Train* by Donald Crews. This part of the center has three activities for the children to complete.

a. A set of train cars, made of laminated construction paper or poster board, are needed. Children are to match the color of the train cars to those in the book. The shape of the train cars should *closely* approximate cars in the book: for example, a red caboose, an orange tank car, a yellow hopper car, etc. The color words should be written in manuscript on the train cars.

b. This exercise extends the difficulty of Activity #1. The shape of the train cars remains the same, but they are all made from white paper or poster board. The color words should be written on the car in the appropriate color. Outline the shape of the car in the correct color also. The children are to match the color words on the cars to the color of the cars in the book.

c. In this activity, the children are given no color cues. The shape of the train cars should again closely correspond to those in the book. The color word should be written on the car in black. The children are to match the color *words* on the cars to the color of the cars in the book.

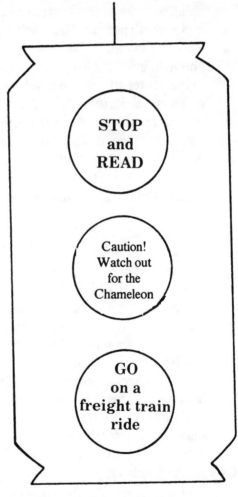

2) The second part of the center is "CAUTION — Watch Out for the Chameleon," based on the book *A Color of His Own* by Leo Lionni. This is a painting station. Paper, paints, and brushes should be available. In the book, a chameleon is depicted in a variety of colors and color combinations. Have the children paint chameleons. Encourage creativity. Display their paintings in the color center.

3) The third part of the center is "STOP and Read." All the activities in this part of the center are based on books. It is not necessary that the children complete every activity suggested. The teacher may choose according to his/her own needs and those of the children.

a. Using the book *Is It Red? Is It Yellow? Is It Blue?* by Tana Hoban, have the children tell stories into a cassette tape recorder. The book is wordless, and the illustrations carry no continuous story line. The children can use individual pages for their stories. The tapes may be placed in the center for others to listen to, or they may be transcribed so that a printed version can accompany the tape.

b. Have the children make a class book like Eric Carle's *My Very First Book of Colors*. The top of each page is a piece of colored construction paper. The children can cut out pictures and paste them on the bottom of the page.

c. Using *Harold and The Purple Crayon* by Crockett Johnson as a stimulus, have the children make a class language experience book of pictures. Each child chooses a color and makes a picture. The teacher labels each picture with a title, such as "Amy and Her Yellow Crayon," "Tom and His Green Crayon," etc. The children dictate a sentence about their picture to the teacher, who writes it at the bottom of the page. Place the book in the center so that the children may look at the pictures and read the sentences.

d. The book *Rain* by Robert Kalan adapts well to a flannel board story which can be incorporated into a partner activity for the center. The objects in the story are simple, colors are named, and the sequence is well-defined: for example, yellow sun, white clouds, red car, etc. With two children working together, one can use the book and direct the other to place the pieces on the flannel board in order. The book is used as the self-check. A blue background is recommended. Raindrops made from waxed paper adhere well to flannel.

e. Using *The Chalk Box Story* by Donald Freeman as the basis for the activity, have the children make colored chalk pictures. Large size artist's chalk works best and comes in a variety of colors. (Chalk pictures are less messy when the paper is dampened before the chalk is applied.) Display the pictures in the center.

f. Group activity: Leo Lionni's *Little Blue and Little Yellow* lends itself well to storytelling by the teacher, using an overhead projector and transparencies. The transparencies allow the children to see how blue and yellow make green. After the teacher has told the story, children can be invited to make up stories about the adventures of other colors such as "Little Blue and Little Red" and "Little Red and Little Yellow." Pieces of transparency film in these colors should be available for the children to manipulate on the overhead. (An inexpensive and easily accessible source of this material is protective plastic covers for research papers which can be purchased at any drug store. These come in red, blue, and yellow.)

Culminating activity:

To serve as an indication that the children have completed the center activities and for assessment purposes, have the children make rainbow badges like this one:

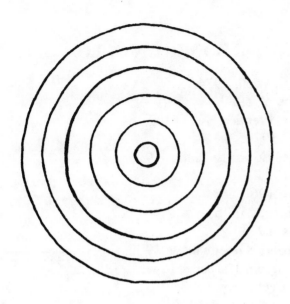

Beginning at the center, the circles follow the sequence of the colors of the rainbow: red, orange, yellow, green, blue, purple.

Have available a box of construction paper circles in six different sizes and colors and some glue. Post a chart with these directions:

Make a rainbow badge.

1. Start with a purple O.
2. Glue a blue O on top.
3. Glue a green O on top.
4. Glue a yellow O on top.
5. Glue an orange O on top.
6. Glue a red O on top.

(Do not use color cues for any of the words on the chart.)

Both colors and color words are reinforced in this activity. If you wish to review only colors and not color words, directions for making the badge may be placed on a cassette tape. Pin the badges on the children and let them wear them.

SELECTED BIBLIOGRAPHY OF BOOKS ON COLOR

Carle, Eric. *My Very First Book of Colors*. Crowell, 1974.

_____. *Let's Paint a Rainbow*. Philomel, 1982.

Chermayeff, Ivan. *Tomato and Other Colors*. Prentice-Hall, 1982.

Crews, Donald. *Freight Train*. Greenwillow, 1978.

Denton, John. *The Color Factory*. Il. by Peter Edwards. Puffin, 1976.

Duvoisin, Roger. *See What I Am*. Lothrop, 1974.

Emberley, Ed. *Green Says Go*. Little, Brown, 1968.

Freeman, Don. *The Chalk Box Story*. Lippincott, 1976.

Haskins, Ilma. *Color Seems*. Vanguard Press, 1973.

Hoban, Tana. *Is It Red? Is It Yellow? Is It Blue?* Greenwillow, 1978.

Johnson, Crockett. *Harold and the Purple Crayon*. Harper & Row, 1958.

Kalan, Robert. *Rain*. Il. by Donald Crews. Greenwillow, 1978.

Lionni, Leo. *Little Blue and Little Yellow*. Astor-Honor, 1959.

_____. *A Color of His Own*. Pantheon, 1975.

O'Neill, Mary. *Hailstones and Halibut Bones*. Il. by Leonard Weisgard. Doubleday, 1961.

Provensen, Martin and Alice. *What is Color?* Golden, 1967.

Reiss, John J. *Colors*. Bradbury, 1969.

Zolotow, Charlotte, *Mr. Rabbit and the Lovely Present*. Il. by Maurice Sendak. Harper & Row, 1962.

SHAPES CENTER

The shapes center has a clown theme. Activities for group work as well as independent work are included. The backdrop of the center is a bulletin board, as shown below.

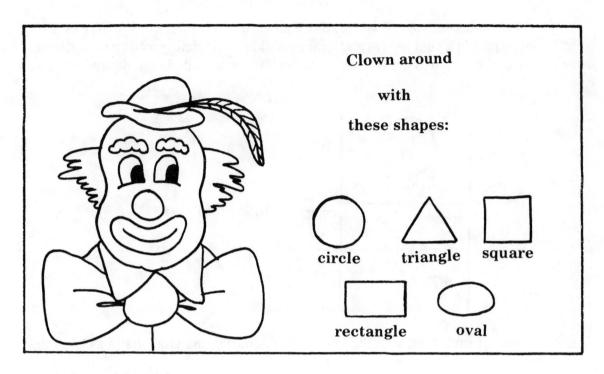

Clown around

with

these shapes:

circle   triangle   square

rectangle   oval

Independent Activities:

1) "Sad Sam" — This card game involves the matching of shapes and is played like "Old Maid." For this game, you need 35 cards: 34 of the cards are matched pairs, and one card is "Sad Sam." These shapes are suggested for the cards: circle, triangle, square, rectangle, oval, crescent, heart, diamond, star, cross, clover, arrow, half-moon, cone, zero, octagon (stop sign), zig zag. (See sample cards).

To play, all the cards are shuffled and dealt to the players. Each player draws one card from the hand of the player to his/her right. Players lay down matching pairs for all to see. Drawing and matching continue until one player is left holding "Sad Sam."

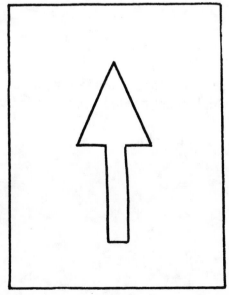

SAD SAM

SAMPLE CARDS (actual size)

2) Have the children make a book like Eric Carle's *My Very First Book of Shapes*. Cut out a shape and paste it to the top page and have the children find pictures of objects that have that shape and paste them to the bottom page. Do this for any number of desired shapes. Example:

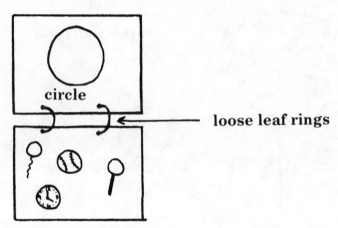

Later, the teacher may work with the children individually and label the objects on the bottom page.

3) "Spin A Clown" game. For this game you need a die, a spinner, 4 clown game boards, and a collection of shapes. The spinner should be made as shown in the illustration. A small cardboard pizza round would make a sturdy base. (See Chapter 2 for directions for making spinners.)

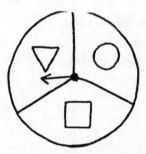

The 4 game boards (as shown on next page 140) should be made from heavy posterboard. Laminated construction paper shapes in different colors are needed to correspond to the appropriate areas on the game board clown:

   7 circles (2 eyes, 1 nose, 3 buttons, 1 at top of hat)
   5 triangles (2 arms, 2 legs, 1 hat)
   1 square (body)

There will need to be enough shapes to complete 4 clowns (28 circles, 20 triangles, 4 squares). Up to four children may play. Each child receives a game board. Shapes should be randomly scattered about the playing area. A roll of the die determines who goes first. One at a time, players spin for shapes to cover areas on the clown. If a player has covered all of one kind of shape on the clown and spins that shape again, he/she automatically misses a turn. The first player to complete his/her clown wins the game. There is no specific order of placement of shapes on the clown, other than the obvious one: the body square must placed before the button circles. Color is not a consideration; any combination of colored shapes will do. When making the gameboards, the entire outline of the clown should be drawn. Areas that are not to be covered with shapes should be colored in.

4) To reinforce the concepts of "circle" and "round," have the children make "Cheerios" pictures. For this activity, you will need to supply paper, glue, and Cheerios in the station. Display finished pictures in the center.

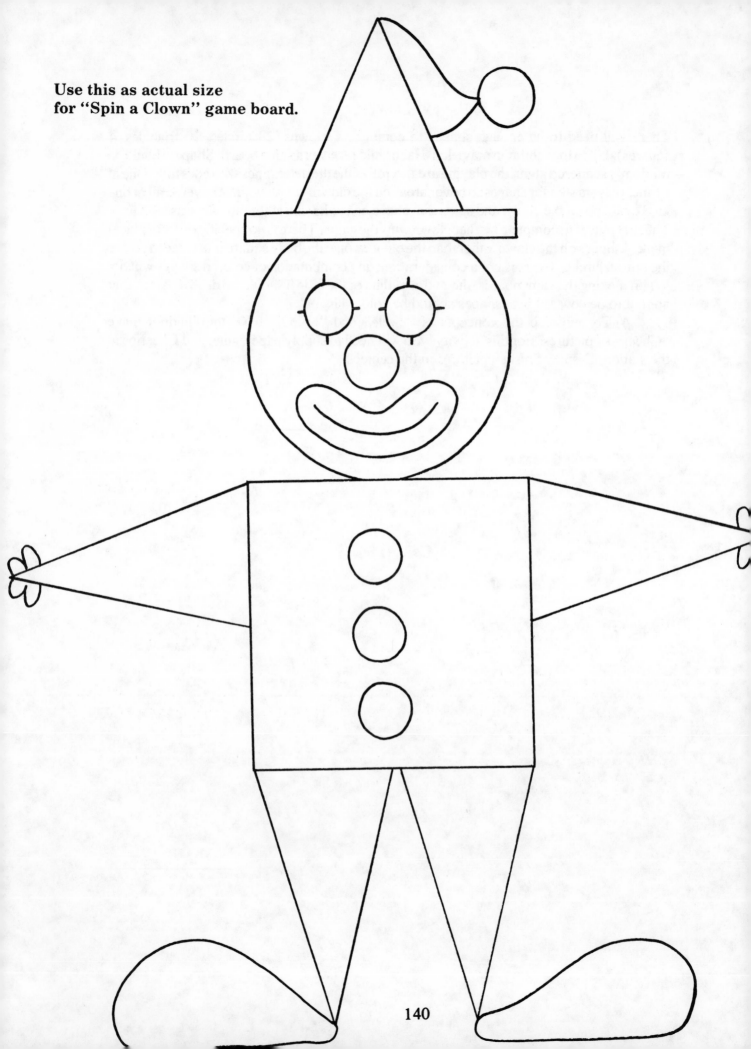

Use this as actual size
for "Spin a Clown" game board.

140

Group Activities:

1) **Paper Plate Clown Puppet.** These materials are needed: 1½ paper plates per puppet, an assortment of shapes, yarn, glue, and a stapler. The features on the face of the clown are made from various shapes. It is recommended that these shapes be pre-cut or stenciled for the children to cut out. See illustration below. DIRECTIONS: The clown face is the *back* of the paper plate, not the eating surface. Put facial features on first. (Eyes are made of two parts; the triangle is glued on first.) Then staple the *half* plate to the back of the top of the whole plate. The plates should be stapled edge to edge, eating surfaces together. This leaves an opening in which a child can insert his/her hand to hold the puppet. The square for the hat should be glued on next, overlapping the top of the paper plate. The rectangular hat's brim is next. The ears are circles which are glued onto the back so that only half the circle is visible from the front. The ruffle is a series of five ovals glued onto the back of the puppet. Pieces of yarn glued on for hair complete the puppet.

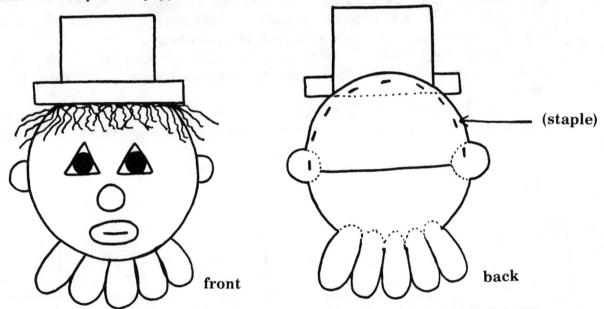

front   (staple)   back

2) Take a walk around the school and in the neighborhood. Look for shapes in the environment. Take black and white photographs and make a class book like Hoban's *Circles, Triangles, and Squares*.

3) Make language experience shape books. The shape of the book is the shape being studied, as illustrated below:

141

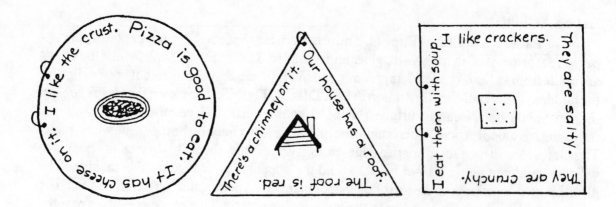

For each page, children find a picture, paste it in the center of the page, and dictate some sentences about the picture. Pages are put together to make a book.

4) Have children collect small objects of various shapes and display them. Have some books available, such as *Shapes* by Reiss, to help them with ideas.

5) Collect objects which have definite outlines, such as those in Hoban's *Shapes and Things*. Use an overhead projector to show the outline and have the children identify the objects.

6) Make triangular hats. Materials needed: paper cut 18 x 15 inches, a stapler, and odds and ends for decorating. (Newspaper, wrapping paper, etc., work very well.) DIRECTIONS: Fold the paper in half, crosswise. Fold corners A and B to meet in the center. Then fold up bottom edges. Spread open hat. Overlap ends and staple each end. Ready to wear!

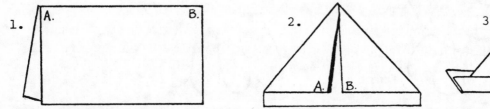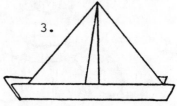

The children might want to decorate the hats with yarn, ric rac, buttons, pompoms, glitter, ribbon, etc.

7) Involve the whole class in games and activities that make use of shapes, such as games in which the children have to form a circle to play. Have the children do action rhymes like the one that follows:

I can make a circle big and round. (Make a big circle with arms.)

I can make it bounce up and down. (Make a bouncing motion with hand.)

I can make a triangle, one, two, three. (Put up left index finger, join it at top with right index finger, connect thumbs for base of triangle.)

I can make it be a hat for me. (Put triangle on top of head.)

If I have 4 sides, I can make a square. (Begin with index finger of both hands together; move them out, down, and back in to form a square.)

It can be like *big* blocks that I stack high in the air. (Using both hands, children pretend to stack blocks, stretching to reach the top of the stack.)

I can make a rectangle long and tall. (Trace rectangular shape in the air with index finger.)

I can open it like a door and go into the hall. (Make motion of opening a door and take 1 step forward.)

8) Obtain some triangles (musical instruments) and have the children experiment with rhythms.

9) Bake shape cookies using any recipe for rolled cookies or the one suggested below:

SHAPE COOKIES:

1¾ cups flour
½ teaspoon baking powder
¼ teaspoon salt
½ cup shortening
¾ cup sugar
1 well-beaten egg
¾ teaspoon vanilla

Cream shortening, add sugar and continue to beat until light. Add well-beaten egg and vanilla. Sift baking powder, salt, and flour. Add dry ingredients to creamed mixture. Mix all thoroughly and chill. Roll on lightly floured board and cut out desired shapes. Bake in 400° oven for 6-10 minutes. *Makes about 3 dozen cookies.*

10) Clown Mobile. These materials are needed:

yarn in two sizes: 12-inch pieces and 3-inch pieces

crayons

glue

precut construction paper shapes:

2 large circles, 7 inches in diameter

2 smaller circles, 3½ inches in diameter

2 triangles, 3 inches on each side

2 rectangles, 4½ x 1 inch

6 ovals, 4½ inches in length

small circles for buttons and one for the top of the hat

Assemble the mobile as shown in the illustrations. The yarn is sandwiched (glued) between the shapes so that the clown has a front and back side.

1. Arrange shapes in order. Place long piece of yarn on top and glue. Glue both shorter pieces of yarn in place for legs.

2. Glue corresponding shapes on top.

3. Glue on arms, buttons, and circle at top of hat. Children may design a face for their clown with crayons.

SELECTED BIBLIOGRAPHY OF BOOKS ON SHAPES

Adler, David A. *Three-D, Two-D*. Crowell, 1975.

Atwood, Ann. *The Little Circle*. Scribner, 1967.

Brown, Marcia Joan. *Listen to a Shape*. Watts, 1979.

Budney, Blossom. *A Kiss is Round*. Lothrop, 1954.

Carle, Eric. *My Very First Book of Shapes*. Crowell, 1974.

Emberley, Ed. *A Wing on a Flea, A Book About Shapes*. Little, Brown, 1961.

Friskey, Margaret. *Three Sides and the Round One*. Children's Press, 1973.

Froman, Robert. *Angles are as Easy as Pie*. Crowell, 1975.

Hoban, Tana. *Circles, Triangles and Squares*. Macmillan, 1974.

——————. *Shapes and Things*. Macmillan, 1970.

——————. *Round & Round & Round*. Greenwillow, 1983.

Kahn, Bernice. *Everything Has a Shape and Everything Has a Size*. Prentice-Hall, 1964.

Kessler, Ethel and Leonard. *Are You Square?* Doubleday, 1966.

Reiss, John J. *Shapes*. Bradbury, 1974.

Schlein, Miriam. *Shapes*. Scott, 1952.

Sitomer, Mindel and Harry. *What is Symmetry?* Crowell, 1970.

Tester, Sylvia. *The Parade of Shapes*. Children's Press, 1976.

Informational Books

SCIENCE   Animal Kingdom

The learning center suggested here deals with the teaching of insects. Many of the activities, however, can be adapted to other areas of natural science. Well-illustrated informational books are an important part of the center. Although many primary grade children may not be able to read the books themselves, the illustrations will be helpful for developing concepts. Books should be read aloud to the children as well. An extensive bibliography is included at the end of this chapter.

Independent Activities:

1) **Bulletin board riddles.** This bulletin board is a participation activity in which the children match descriptive riddles with pictures. Pictures should be photographs or drawings that are as realistic as possible. Sources of pictures include *Ranger Rick* magazine, published by the National Wildlife Federation, and *World* magazine, published by the National Geographic Society, and other publications from these two organizations. Teachers should also check the school media center for available Study Prints on various topics. Riddles may be written on index cards. Books should be available for reference.

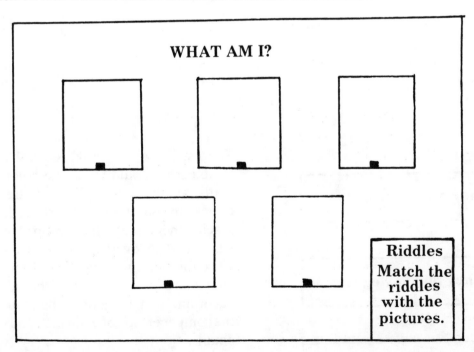

Children are to read the riddles and match them with the appropriate pictures. Putting a piece of Velcro on the bottom of each picture and on the back of each riddle card is an excellent way to attach the two. All riddle cards should be kept in a large envelope attached to the bulletin board. An answer key should be provided. Pictures and riddles may be changed often. After a while, some children may want to locate pictures and write riddles for the bulletin board themselves.

Sample riddles:

I am very small.	I have a hard shell.
I live in a colony.	I like to eat aphids.
I leave a trail to food.	I can fly.
What am I? (ant)	What am I? (ladybug)
When I am a baby, I am a caterpillar.	I am a very bright color.
I hatch from a cocoon.	I have large wings.
I can fly.	I live near water.
What am I? (butterfly)	What am I? (dragonfly)

2) **Topic-Details Sort.** In this activity, children match informational details to topic headings.

Suggested size for cards is 1 x 4 inches. All topic cards should be of one color; all detail cards, another color. Children are to lay the topic cards on a table and sort the detail cards, placing them under the appropriate headings. Cards that go together should be coded on the back for self-checking. Detail cards that fit with more than one topic should be coded accordingly. This activity helps to reinforce the compehension of main idea and supporting details.

> **Spiders**

> **They are not insects**

> **They may lay eggs**

> **They spin webs**

Directions:
Write the answer to each question in the spots. Use the words at the bottom of the page to help you. Check you work with the answer sheet. For each right answer, color the spot black. Color the ladybug red.

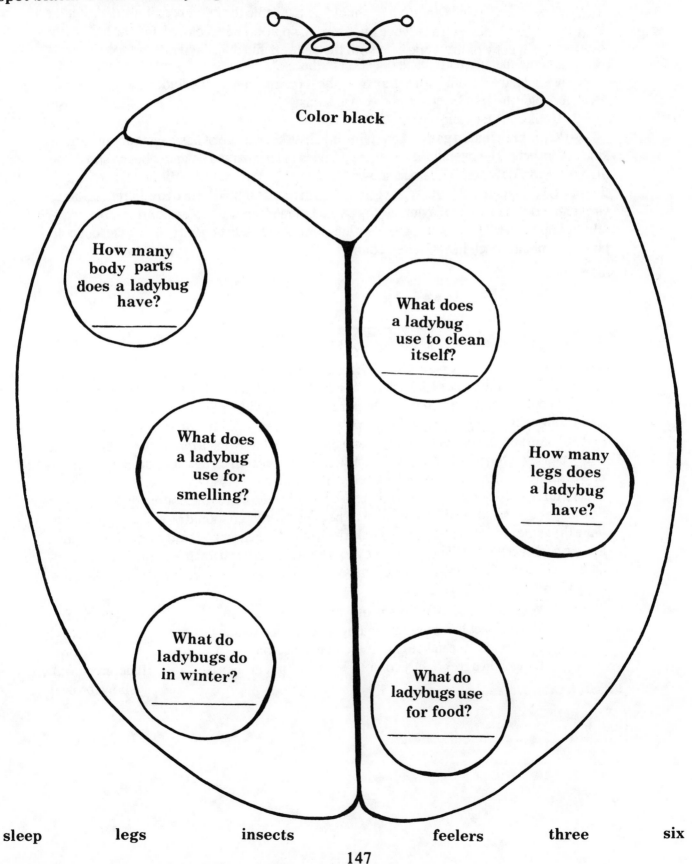

Color black

How many body parts does a ladybug have?
_____

What does a ladybug use to clean itself?
_____

What does a ladybug use for smelling?
_____

How many legs does a ladybug have?
_____

What do ladybugs do in winter?
_____

What do ladybugs use for food?
_____

sleep   legs   insects   feelers   three   six

147

3) **Ladybug Worksheet.** The worksheet has questions about ladybugs, one on each spot. Children are to write in the answers to the questions. Hawes' *Ladybug, Ladybug, Fly Away Home* or McClung's *Ladybug* should be available for reference, if needed. Put the worksheets in a folder with a ladybug on the front, appropriately colored. On the back of the folder, have a copy of the worksheet with the answers filled in. Students are to:
    a. write the answer to each question in the spots
    b. check their work with the answer sheet on the back of the folder
    c. color the spot black for each correct answer
    d. color the ladybug red

4) **Comprehension game.** This game involves knowledge of basic facts about various kinds of insects. The overall theme of the game is caterpillars. The game board should be made of heavy duty poster board as shown on page 151. Two sets of cards are needed: question cards and game cards. Question cards and game cards should be of two different colors to eliminate confusion. The playing pieces can be made from pom poms to resemble caterpillars. Glue four ½" pom poms onto a two inch strip of felt. Add tiny felt eyes. Make four pom pom caterpillars, each in a different color.

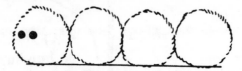

Directions for playing:

Two to four children may play. Children spin for a caterpillar playing piece color and to see who begins the game. The spinner should be divided into four sections. Each section should be color coded to match the colors of the pom pom caterpillars. (See Chapter 2 for directions for making spinners.) All pom pom caterpillars are placed on the head to begin the game. The player who spins the highest number starts the game by drawing a *question* card. If he/she answers the question correctly, he/she draws a *game* card which instructs the player how to move on the game board caterpillar's body. If he/she answers incorrectly, the next player takes a turn. Used question cards and game cards are returned to the bottom of the pile. The first player to reach the tail is the winner of the game. Children should be encouraged to continue the game until all players have reached the tail. An answer key card should be provided in case of disagreement. The answer key will be easier to use if each question card is numbered so that the child who is "judge" can quickly locate the correct answer. Sample questions for question cards:

What insect usually lives near water?	(dragonfly)
What insect has a very long tongue to use for sucking nectar?	(butterfly)
How many queen bees are there in each colony?	(one)
Dragonflies are brightly colored. What colors can they be?	(blue, green, red, yellow, brown)

What insect sits on the egg-cell and helps keep the egg warm?   (honeybee)
How many body parts does an insect have?   (three)
How many legs does an insect have?   (six)
What insect can fly at a speed up to 60 miles per hour?   (dragonfly)
What are the three kinds of bees?   (queen, worker, drone)
What insect looks like a stick with legs?   (a walkingstick)
What do insects use their antennae for?   (smell and touch)
How many wings do most insects have?   (four)
Where is honey made?   (in the bee's stomach)
What is the comb inside a beehive made of?   (wax)
How do ladybugs clean themselves?   (with their legs)
All ladybugs are females — yes or no?   (no)
How many legs does a spider have?   (eight)
What two kinds of insects have a *queen*?   (bee, ant)

How many stomachs does an ant have?   (two)
How is a mosquito like a fly?   (they both have just two wings)
What insect do people think brings good luck?   (ladybug)

This is a starter list of questions. Delete or add others to fit the topics being studied.
Sample game cards:

A friendly child has just give you a ride ahead two spaces on his finger.

Some ants have asked you to enjoy a picnic with them. Stay on your space and eat!

A snail has asked you to go for a walk. *Slowly* move to the next space.

A woodpecker has just decided that you will be his dinner. Head for cover and move back one space.

Oh, no! You have just caught one antenna in a spider's web. Go back one space.

There is a boy just ahead waiting for you with a big stick. Stay on your space.

Look out! Here comes the farmer with bug spray! Go back one space.

You have just climbed to the end of a very long branch. Take a rest and stay on your space.

A bee has just landed on your leaf. Watch out for that stinger and move ahead two spaces.

You have just met your caterpillar cousin. Stop and visit for a while. Stay on your space.

The leaf you are crawling on in really a turtle. Ride with him to the next space.

You have just met your friend the grasshopper and he gave you a free hop to the next space.

You have just been voted the "most likely to be a beautiful butterfly." You are very happy. Go ahead two spaces.

A curious dog has just flipped you up in the air. Get ready for a crash landing and go back one space.

Oops! You have just fallen into a big puddle. Swim to the top and go back two spaces.

A flock of hungry birds are ahead. Go back to the beginning and wait for another turn.

The twig you are crawling on has turned out to be a snake. Get off fast and go back two spaces.

The wind just blew the leaf you are crawling on ahead two spaces. You may move the two spaces.

Stop and help your caterpillar friend build his cocoon. Stay on your space.

Take a big bite from a bright green leaf and move ahead one space.

Lucky you! You have just escaped being run over by a bicycle. Go ahead two spaces.

Scattered throughout the game cards are special "caterpillar" cards which have the children perform some sort of action:

Use this sample as the model for a large game board.

CATERPILLAR

Directions:
Spin for a caterpillar color.
Place caterpillars on the head.
Highest number begins the game.
Draw a *question card*. Read your card aloud and answer the question.

If you answer correctly, draw a *game card* and do what it says.
If you do not answer correctly, the next player takes a turn.
All question and game cards are returned to the bottom of the pile.
First player to reach the tail wins the game.
Play until *everyone* reaches the tail.

Question cards

Game cards

Spinner

151

Clap your hands three times.
Walk very quietly to the window. Then come back and sit down.
Stand up. Do five jumping jacks.
Stand up. Bend over and touch your toes five times.
Stand up and turn around three times.
Shake hands with all the other players.

What are the
three kinds of
bees?

QUESTION CARD

A snail has asked
you to go for a walk.
Slowly move to the
next space.

GAME CARD

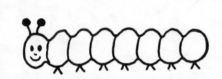

Clap your hands
three times.

CATERPILLAR CARD

5) **Label Body Parts.** Put the drawings on page 153 on a piece of tagboard. Put labels for the various body parts on individual cards. Children are to put the cards in the correct places. Provide a correctly labeled drawing for checking.

6) Using *A Dog's Book of Bugs* by Griffen as a stimulus, have the children write concrete poetry (see Chapter 6) about various insects. This book looks at insects from a dog's point of view. For another activity, have the children write stories about insects from the viewpoint of another animal.

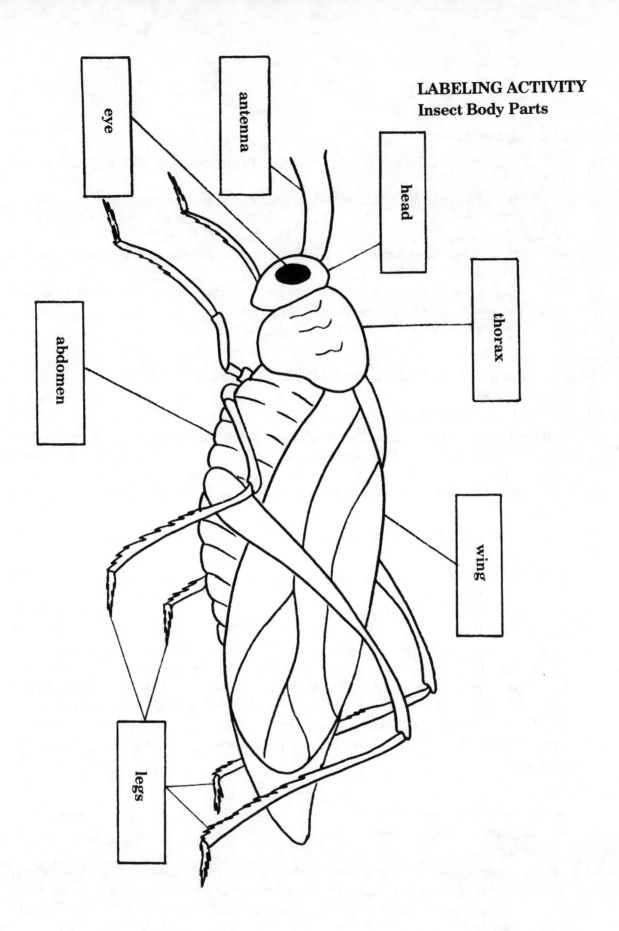

LABELING ACTIVITY
Insect Body Parts

eye

antenna

head

thorax

abdomen

wing

legs

Group Activities:

1) Involve the children in simple research activities on topics such as "How Insects Help Us."

2) *Which is Which?* by Russell charts comparisons between pairs of a variety of animals. Two sections compare butterflies with moths and bees with wasps. Have the children develop similar comparisons between other kinds of insects.

3) If possible, collect display materials for the center, including a butterfly collection, an ant farm, cocoons, honeycomb, etc.

4) Take a field trip to visit a beekeeper, or have one come into the classroom to talk with the children about caring for bees and gathering honey.

5) Do some cooking with honey. Suggested recipes:

* EASY HONEY CANDY

¼ cup honey	1 cup finely chopped nuts
½ cup butter or margarine	½ teaspoon vanilla

Heat a 1-quart casserole until very hot. Melt butter in it. Add nuts and vanilla. Stir together until the nuts are well coated with the butter. Add the honey and beat again until thoroughly mixed. Refrigerate. When the mixture is cool enough to handle, shape it into balls a tablespoon at a time. With the candies not touching, store in the refrigerator. Yield: 15-18 pieces.

* HONEY GINGERBREAD COOKIES

½ cup sugar	2 teaspoons cinnamon
3 cups sifted flour	½ teaspoon nutmeg
2 teaspoons baking soda	1 cup butter or margarine, cut into dots
1 teaspoon salt	½ cup honey
2 teaspoons ginger	½ teaspoon cloves

Sift the sugar, flour, baking soda, salt, ginger, cinnamon, cloves, and nutmeg together into a mixing bowl. Work the dots of butter into the dry ingredients with your fingertips. When butter is thoroughly worked in, add the honey and stir until blended. Refrigerate for an hour or longer. Roll the dough out about ⅛-inch thick on a floured board. Cut out shapes of gingerbread men. Bake for 12-15 minutes in a preheated 350° oven. Yield: about 2½ dozen.

The Pooh Book by Virginia Ellison (E.P. Dutton, 1969) contains many recipes for cooking with honey.

POPCORN BALLS

3 quarts popped popcorn (salt free)
½ cup honey

Pour popped popcorn into a large bowl. Put honey into a small saucepan. Bring to a boil over low heat and simmer for 10 minutes. Pour honey over the popcorn and, with a pair of forks, begin to toss the popcorn gently, to get as much of it covered with honey as you can. When just cool enough to handle, press handfuls together into balls. Yield: depends on the size of the balls.

6) **Bee Paper Bag Puppet.** Materials needed are a paper bag (lunch bag size), yellow and black construction paper, black pipe cleaners, and glue. Pieces are glued into place as follows:

Glue black pipe cleaner antennae into place on the "flap" as shown. Then glue the head, made from yellow construction paper, on top. Body is yellow construction paper with black construction paper stripes. Legs are black construction paper. Glue legs on first; then body on top. Glue yellow construction paper wings on the back of the bag, as shown in the drawing. Children may put on facial features with crayons. Eyes should be very large.

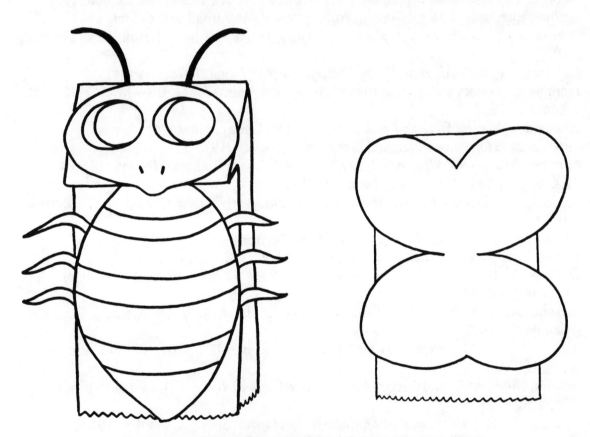

SELECTED BIBLIOGRAPHY OF BOOKS
ON INSECTS & SPIDERS

Allen, Gertrude. *Everyday Insects*. Houghton, 1963.

Bernard, George. *Dragonflies*. (Oxford Scientific Films). Putnam, 1980.

Chenery, Janet. *Wolfie*. Il. by Marc Simont. Harper & Row, 1969.

Cloudsley-Thompson, J.L. *Spiders and Scorpions*. Il. by Joyce Bee. McGraw-Hill, 1974.

Cole, Joanna. *Find the Hidden Insect*. Il. by Jerome Wexler. Morrow, 1979.

Conklin, Gladys. *When Insects are Babies*. Il. by Arthur Marokvia. Holiday, 1969.

_____. *Insects Build Their Homes* Il. by Jean Zallinger. Holiday, 1972.

_____. *I Like Beetles*. Il. by Jean Zallinger. Holiday, 1975.

_____. *Praying Mantis*. Il. by Glen Rounds. Holiday, 1978.

Cooke, John. *The Butterfly Cycle*. (Oxford Scientific Films). Putnam, 1977.

_____. *The Spider's Web*. (Oxford Scientific Films). Putnam, 1978.

Darby, Gene. *Jerry Finds Spiders*. Il by Joe Nerlinger. Steck-Vaughn, 1969.

Freschet, Berniece. *The Web in the Grass*. Il. by Roger Duvoisin. Scribner, 1972.

George, Jean Craighead. *All Upon a Sidewalk*. Il. by Don Bolognese. Dutton, 1974.

Griffen, Elizabeth. *A Dog's Book of Bugs*. Il. by Peter Parnall. Atheneum, 1967.

Hawes, Judy. *Ladybug, Ladybug, Fly Away Home*. Il. by Ed Emberley. Crowell, 1967.

Hoberman, Mary Ann. *Bugs*. Il. by Victoria Chess. Viking, 1976. (poems)

Hornblow, Leonora and Arthur. *Insects Do the Strangest Things*. Il. by Michael K. Frith. Random, 1968.

Huntington, Harriet E. *Let's Look at Insects*. Doubleday, 1969.

Lecht, Jane. *Honeybees*. National Geographic Society, 1973.

Marcher, Marion W. *Monarch Butterfly*. Il. by Barbara Latham. Holiday, 1960.

McClung, Robert M. *Ladybug*. Morrow, 1966.

_____. *Green Darner, the Story of a Dragonfly*. Il. by Carol Lerner. Morrow, 1980.

Overbeck, Cynthia. *The Butterfly Book*. Il. by Sharon Lerner. Lerner, 1978.

Patent, Dorothy Hinshaw. *Spider Magic*. Holiday, 1982.

Sammis, Kathy. *The Beginning Knowledge Book of Butterflies*. Il. by Paul Lipp. Macmillan, 1965.

Selsam, Millicent E. *Questions and Answers About Ants*. Il. by Arabelle Wheatley. Scholastic, 1967.

_____. *Where Do They Go? Insects in Winter*. Il. by Arabelle Wheatley. Four Winds, 1982.

Selsam, Millicent E. and Joyce Hunt. *A First Look at Insects*. Il. by Harriett Springer. Walker, 1974.

_____. *A First Look at Spiders*. Il. by Harriett Springer. Walker, 1983.

Sheehan, Angela. *The Bumblebee*. Il. by Maurice Pledger. Warwick, 1976.

Thompson, David. *Bees and Honey*. (Oxford Scientific Films). Putnam, 1976.

Wagner, Jenny *Aranea· A Story About a Spider*. Il. by Ron Brooks. Bradbury, 1978.

Whitlock, Ralph, *A Closer Look at Butterflies and Moths*. Il. by Norman Weaver, Tony Swift, Philip Weare. Gloucester Press, 1978.

SELECTED BIBLIOGRAPHY OF BOOKS ON ANIMALS

Adamson, Joy. *Elsa*. Pantheon, 1963.

Alston, Eugenia. *Come Visit a Prairie Dog Town*. Il. by St. Tamara. Harcourt, 1976.

Arnold, Caroline. *Five Nests*. Il. by Ruth Sanderson. Dutton, 1980.

Arnosky, Jim. *A Kettle of Hawks and Other Wildlife Groups*. Coward, 1979.

Aruego, Jose. *Symbiosis*. Scribner, 1970.

Behrens, June. *Whale Watch!* Children's Press, 1978.

Bernard, George. *The Wild Rabbit*. (Oxford Scientific Films). Putnam, 1980.

Bevans, Michael H. *The Book of Sea Shells*. Doubleday, 1961.

Blassingame, Wyatt. *Porcupines*. Dodd, 1982.

Bonners, Susan. *Panda*. Delacorte, 1978.

_____. *A Penguin Year*. Delacorte, 1981.

Brady, Irene. *Beaver Year*. Houghton, 1976.

Bridge, Linda McCarter. *Cats*. National Geographic Society, 1974.

Busch, Phyllis S. *At Home in Its Habitat, Animal Neighborhoods*. Il. by Arline Strong. World, 1970.

Carrick, Carol. *Sand Tiger Shark*. Il. by Donald Carrick. Seabury, 1977.

_____. *Octopus*. Il. by Donald Carrick. Seabury, 1978.

Clayton, J.M. *All Color Book of Seashells*. Octopus Books, 1974 (USA: Crown).

Cole, Joanna. *My Puppy is Born*. Il. by Jerome Wexler. Morrow, 1973.

_____. *A Calf is Born*. Il. by Jerome Wexler. Morrow, 1975.

_____. *A Bird's Body*. Il. by Jerome Wexler. Morrow, 1982.

Cole, Joanna and Jerome Wexler. *A Chick Hatches*. Morrow, 1976.

_____. *A Fish Hatches*. Morrow, 1978.

Cousteau, Jacques-Yves. *The Art of Motion (The Ocean World of Jacques Cousteau)*. World, 1973.

Craig, M. Jean. *Little Monsters*. Dial, 1977.

Darling, Lois and Louis. *Worms*. Morrow, 1972.

Deguine, Jean-Claude. *Emperor Penguin*. Stephen Greene Press, 1974.

de Paola, Tomie. *The Kid's Cat Book*. Holiday, 1979.

Fisher, Aileen. *But Ostriches. .* Il. by Peter Parnall. Crowell, 1970.

Foster, Joanna. *Dogs Working for People*. Il. by James Stanfield. National Geographic Society, 1972.

Fox, Michael W. and Wende Devlin Gates. *What is Your Cat Saying?* Coward, 1982.

Freedman, Russell. *Hanging On, How Animals Carry Their Young*. Holiday, 1977.

Freschet, Berniece. *Turtle Pond*. Il. by Donald Carrick. Scribner, 1971.

_____. *Bear Mouse*. Il. by Donald Carrick. Scribner, 1973.

_____. *Skunk Baby*. Il. by Kazue Mizumura. Crowell, 1973.

Friedman, Judi. *The Eels' Strange Journey*. Il. by Gail Owens. Crowell, 1976.

Gabb, Michael H. *Creatures Great and Small*. Lerner, 1980.

Gans, Roma. *Bird Talk*. Il. by Jo Polseno. Crowell, 1971.

Garelick, Mary. *About Owls*. Il. by Tony Chen. Holt, 1978.

_____. *It's About Birds*. Il by Tony Chen. Holt, 1978.

Goudey, Alice E. *Houses From the Sea*. Il. by Adrienne Adams. Scribner, 1959.

Gross, Ruth Belov. *What is that Alligator Saying?* Il. by John Hawkinson. Hastings, 1972.

_____. *A Book About Pandas*. Dial, 1972.

_____. *Alligators and Other Crocodilians*. Four Winds, 1976.

Grosvenor, Donna K. *Pandas*. National Geographic Society, 1973.

Hawes, Judy. *Why Frogs are Wet*. Il. by Don Madden. Crowell, 1968.

Hess, Lilo. *The Amazing Earthworm*. Scribner, 1979.

_____. *The Diary of a Rabbit*. Scribner, 1982.

Hunt, Patricia. *Koalas*. Dodd, 1980.

_____. *Snowy Owls*. Dodd, 1982.

Hurd, Edith Thacher. *The Mother Beaver*. Il. by Clement Hurd. Little, Brown, 1971.

_____. *The Mother Deer*. Il. by Clement Hurd. Little, Brown, 1972.

_____. *The Mother Whale*. Il. by Clement Hurd. Little, Brown, 1973.

_____. *The Mother Owl*. Il. by Clement Hurd. Little, Brown, 1974.

_____. *The Mother Kangaroo*. Il. by Clement Hurd. Little, Brown, 1976.

_____. *The Mother Chimpanzee*. Il. by Clement Hurd. Little, Brown, 1978.

Isenbart, Hans-Heinrich. *A Duckling is Born*. Trans. by Catherine Edwards Sadler. Il. by Othmar Baumli. Putnam, 1981.

Kane, Henry B. *Wings, Legs, or Fins (How Animals Move From Here to There)*. Knopf, 1965.

LaBastille, Anne. *White-Tailed Deer*. National Wildlife Federation, 1973.

Lauber, Patricia. *Who Needs Alligators?* Garrard. 1974.

_____. *What's Hatching Out of That Egg?* Crown, 1979.

McClung, Robert M. *Horseshoe Crab*. Morrow, 1967.

_____. *How Animals Hide*. National Geographic Society, 1973.

_____. *Sea Star*. Morrow, 1975.

_____. *Animals That Build Their Homes*. National Geographic Society, 1976.

McDearmon, Kay. *A Day in the Life of a Sea Otter*. Dodd, 1973.

_____. *Gorillas*. Dodd, 1979.

McGovern, Ann. *Little Whale*. Il by John Hamberger. Four Winds, 1979.

_____. *Sharks*. Il. by Murray Tinkelman. Four Winds, 1976.

Miller, Jane. *Birth of a Foal*. Lippincott, 1977.

_____. *Lambing Time*. Methuen, 1978.

Misumura, Kazue. *The Blue Whale*. Crowell, 1971.

_____. *Opossum*. Crowell, 1974.

Naden, Corinne J. *Let's Find Out About Frogs*. Il. by Jerry Lang. Watts, 1972.

National Geographic Society. *Lion Cubs*. National Geographic Society, 1972.

_____. *Creepy Crawly Things, Reptiles and Amphibians*. National Geographic Society, 1974.

Overbeck, Cynthia. *The Fish Book*. Il. by Sharon Lerner. Lerner, 1978.

Pringle, Laurence. *Twist, Wiggle, and Squirm, a Book About Earthworms*. Il. by Peter Parnall. Crowell, 1973.

Rand, Austin L. *Birds in Summer*. Il. by Edwin Huff. Encyclopedia Britannica Press, 1962.

Russell, Solveig P. *Which is Which?* Il. by Gail Haley. Prentice-Hall, 1966.

Saunders, John R. *Young Animals*. Il. by Corinne and Robert Borja. Children's Press, 1967.

Schoenherr, John. *The Barn*. Little, Brown, 1968.

Schwartz, Elizabeth and Charles. *When Animals are Babies*. Il. by Charles Schwartz. Holiday, 1964.

_____. *When Flying Animals are Babies*. Il. by Charles Schwartz. Holiday, 1973.

Selsam, Millicent E. *How Puppies Grow*. Il. by Esther Bubley. Four Winds, 1971.

Selsam, Millicent E. and Joyce Hunt. *A First Look at Animals Without Backbones*. Il. by Harriett Springer. Walker, 1976.

_____. *A First Look at Frogs, Toads and Salamanders*. Il. by Harriett Springer. Walker, 1976.

Shackelford, Nina and Gordon E. Burks. *Bird Nests*. Il. by James G. Irving. Golden Press, 1962.

Simon, Seymour. *Birds on Your Street*. Il. by Jean Zallinger. Holiday, 1974.

_____. *Animal Fact/Animal Fable*. Il. by Diane de Groat. Crown, 1979.

_____. *Little Giants*. Il. by Pamela Carroll. Morrow, 1983.

Thompson, David. *House Mouse*. (Oxford Scientific Films). Putnam, 1978.

Tresselt, Alvin. *The Beaver Pond*. Il. by Roger Duvoisin. Lothrop, 1970.

Van Wormer, Joe. *Squirrels*. Dutton, 1978.

Weaver, John L. *Grizzly Bears*. Dodd, 1982.

Wild Wild World of Animals. *Beavers and Other Pond Dwellers*. Time-Life Films, 1977.

Wong, Herbert H. and Matthew F. Vessel. *My Snail*. Il. by Jean D. Zallinger. Addison-Wesley, 1976.

Zarchy, Harry. *Sea Shells*. World, 1966.

CHAPTER EIGHT

Reading
Readiness

Children at the readiness level are in need of activities that will enhance and generate the following: cognitive development, language development, sensory development and concept development. Manipulative tasks have been devised in this chapter that will aid in the growth of these areas.

It is also recommended that children be given the opportunity to make free choices among tasks. A large variety of tasks is provided herein to facilitate choice of activities based on need, length of time available and ability of the students involved. There is also opportunity for children to work individually, in small groups, or with the teacher.

This chapter contains suggestions for counting and numeral learning, alphabet, and nursery rhyme centers. Extensive bibliographies of books to use with children in each of these areas are included after each section.

Children at the readiness level probably will not be able to follow written directions. In some cases, pictures or symbols might be appropriate for explaining the activity. Directions may also be placed on a cassette tape, and a tape recorder may be placed in the center. In all situations, children should be "walked through" the center and each activity should be explained to them before they work in the center.

Counting Books

1) Have a variety of manipulatives (blocks, pencils, paper clips, miniature toys, etc.) available in the center for children to handle. Include a series of numbered shoeboxes covered with colorful contact paper. The children are to count objects and place them in the appropriate boxes. These boxes could also be used for a game with picture cards. Each card has a set of objects pictured on it. Children are to sort the cards into the correct boxes. In addition to counting, children may use the manipulative objects for simple grouping activities.

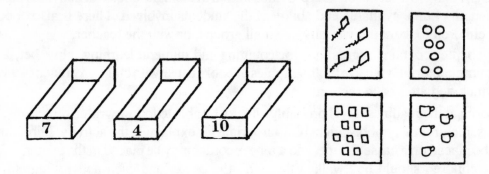

2) Place an abacus in the center for children to use for counting. They may each make an individual abacus by stringing large beads on cord and tying the cord around a piece of heavy cardboard like this:

3) Have a large flannel board in the center and a variety of felt pieces or felt-backed pictures for the children to handle. Make paper cutouts of story characters from appropriate counting books, back them with felt, and let children "tell" the story on the flannel board. For example, *Ten Apples Up On Top* by Theo LeSieg and *The Very Hungry Caterpillar* by Eric Carle adapt well to the flannel board.

4) Make individual-sized flannel boards from squares of cardboard covered with flannel and have available small pieces of felt. Children may want to take these small flannel boards to their seats to use.

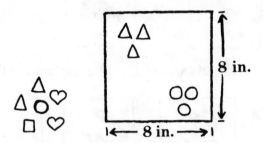

5) Have the children make a large class counting book or one of their own. Use materials of varying textures for the numerals, such as felt, sandpaper, and burlap. Glue one numeral on each page. Then have the children glue a corresponding number of objects on each page. Use buttons, feathers, popcorn, beans, sunflower seeds, beads, gummed stars, plastic rings, stickers (decals), and other small objects for a three-dimensional effect.

6) If possible, get a junior high or high school wood shop class to make a set of numerals from plywood for your class as one of their projects. The children might enjoy painting them. (Always use Latex or some type of washable paint!) Numerals should be about five inches tall.

7) Put cards and markers in the center for "Number Bingo" The child who is caller draws a number card from a container and calls it out. The players look at their cards and cover the numeral if it appears there. The first child to cover all his/her numerals is the winner of the game.

SAMPLE CARDS

4	0
2	8
7	5

9	1	3
7	4	6
5	2	8

8) Set up a "candy store" in the center. Place a toy cash register in the "store." Play candy can be made from styrofoam balls; striped plastic drinking straws may serve as peppermint sticks. Small stones wrapped in colored cellophane and cardboard wrapped in empty candy wrappers may also serve as candy. "Candies" can be put into apothecary-type jars and arranged like a store counter. Many games and activities can be devised using the "candy store." For example, role-playing exercises, in which children have to count out pieces of "candy" for others, can be set up. Children can also learn to count cardboard pennies to pay for their candy. Another idea is to provide a set of cards, each card containing a numeral and a picture of a candy. A child draws a card and then counts out the number of pieces of the candy indicated by the picture and the numeral on the card.

In another activity, children can put cards with candies pictured on them in numerical order.

 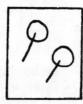 

Or children can play a matching game with the picture cards by matching cards which have the same number of objects.

 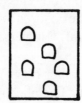    

9) Place cardboard circles or pizza round with numerals or pictures on them in the center. Supply clip-on clothespins. Children are to clip the correct number of clothespins to the circle as indicated by the numeral or pictures.

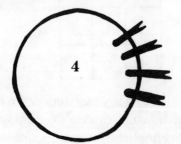 

10) Provide a tape of the song "Over in the Meadow" and at least one of the picture book versions (by Ezra Jack Keats or by John Langstaff and Feodor Rojankovsky). Children can look at the books while listening to the song. This activity might also be a whole group activity, in which the children learn the song. The book may be used as a stimulus for the singing.

11) The sound filmstrip (with cassette) of Maurice Sendak's *One Was Johnny* is available from Weston Woods, Inc. The filmstrip and cassette could be placed in the center for the children's use. A film version of the book is also available from Weston Woods and could be used with the whole group.

12) Place the "Classification Pegboard" activity from page 168 and "Birthday Cake" game from page 169 in the center.

13) Have children make "Teddy Bear Counting Books." See page 170 for directions.

14) Using the book *Max's Toys* by Rosemary Wells as a model, the class can create its own counting book of toys. Children can decide what kind of toy will represent each numeral and then bring in one of their toys to form part of a table display. For example, the class might choose to have *five balls*. Five children would each bring in a ball. Each child can then tell the class about his/her ball and make a picture of it in the counting book. The same thing could be done with *seven cars*, and so on. This activity incorporates oral language, art, and counting. As a final product, the class will have a counting book to which each child has contributed one or more drawings of one of his/her toys. Other skills may evolve from this activity. For example, it is likely that children will bring in different *sizes* of balls, which will offer the opportunity to discuss size and shape. They will probably bring in different types of dolls, cars, trucks, etc., thus allowing for even more discussion of concepts.

1 (red)	2 (blue)	3 (brown)	4 (green)	5 (orange)
☼	🐦🐦	kites	fish	flowers
	🍎🍎			

This classification activity board may be a pegboard with cup hooks or heavy cardboard with stick-on picture hooks. Mount each numeral at the top of each column on a different colored background, as shown. Each card pictures *different* objects. The children are to hang the cards under the correct numeral. The cards may be made self-checking by placing a dot the appropriate color on the back of the card. For example, each card with one object pictured would have a green dot on the back.

Game pieces are small birthday candles
pressed into a ball of clay.

169

Directions for Playing "Birthday Cake"

The game board for "Birthday Cake" is round to represent the top of the cake. (Heavy cardboard cut in a circle or the pizza round of a large pizza would serve as a game board.) Two to four players may play the game. There are two kinds of match cards: those with numerals and those with sets of objects. The cards are placed in two piles, as indicated on the board. Players spin to see who starts the game. The first player draws a card from each pile. If the two cards make a match, i.e., a numeral and the corresponding number of dots, that player spins the spinner and moves his/her candle the number of spaces indicated on the spinner. Cards with a picture of a birthday cake on them should be randomly scattered throughout both piles of cards. If a player draws one of these with another card, it is a "free match" and the player gets to spin. If a player draws two cake cards, he/she gets a double spin. The first player to reach the last space on the cake wins the game.

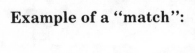  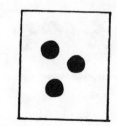

Teddy Bear Counting Book

Using the books *Teddy Bears 1 to 10* by Susanna Gretz and *Ten Bears in my Bed* by Stanley Mack as a stimulus, children can create their own teddy bear counting books.

Have the children cut out a cover to the book from construction paper, using the pattern on the next page, cut so the books will have a teddy bear shape. Then have the children cut out ten pages — one for each numeral from 1 to 10 — for each book, using the same pattern. On each page, the children illustrate what they want the appropriate number of bears to do. They then dictate a sentence about each picture for the teacher to write at the bottom of the page. (See example on next page.)

This activity utilizes the language experience approach. When the counting book is completed, the children will have a book that they can *read* as well as a book which reinforces the number concepts from 1 to 10.

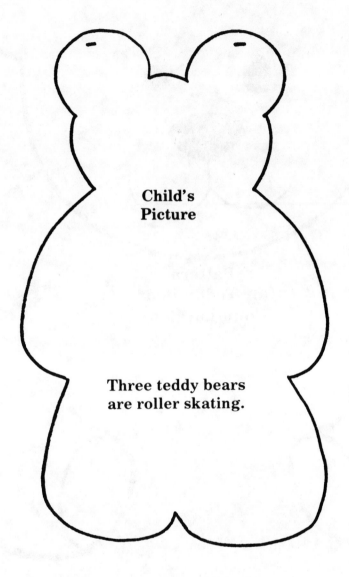

Child's
Picture

Three teddy bears
are roller skating.

Pattern
for Teddy Bear
Counting Book

172

SELECTED BIBLIOGRAPHY OF COUNTING BOOKS

Allen, Robert. *Numbers*. Platt and Munk, 1968.

Anno, Misumasa. *Anno's Counting Book*. Crowell, 1977.

_____. *Anno's Counting House*. Philomel, 1982.

Arnosky, Jim. *Mouse Numbers and Letters*. Harcourt, 1982.

Baker, Jeannie. *One Hungry Spider*. Dutton, 1982.

Bang, Molly. *Ten, Nine, Eight*. Greenwillow, 1983.

Bayley, Nicola. *One Old Oxford Ox*. Atheneum, 1977.

Boynton, Sandra. *Hippo's Go Berserk*. Little, Brown, 1977.

Calmenson, Stephanie. *One Little Monkey*. Il. by Ellen Appleby. Parent's, 1982.

Carle, Eric. *1, 2, 3 to the Zoo*. Collins World, 1969.

_____. *The Very Hungry Caterpillar*. Collins World, 1969.

_____. *What's For Lunch?* Philomel, 1982.

Charles, D. *Count on Calico Cat*. Children's Press, 1974.

Charosh, Mannis. *Number Ideas Through Pictures*. Crowell, 1974.

Chwast, Seymour and Martin Moskof. *Still Another Number Book*. McGraw-Hill, 1971.

Considine, Kate and Ruby Schuler. *One, Two, Three, Four*. Holt, 1963.

Cranston, Margaret. *1, 2, Buckle My Shoe*. Holt, 1967.

Cretan, G.T. *Ten Brothers with Camels*. Golden, 1975.

Crews, Donald. *Ten Black Dots*. Scribner, 1968.

Crowther, Robert. *The Most Amazing Hide-and-Seek Counting Book*. Viking, 1981.

Eichenberg, Fritz. *Dancing on the Moon*. Harcourt, 1955.

Feelings, Muriel. *Moja Means One*. Il. by Tom Feelings. Dial, 1971.

Fehr, Howard. *If You Can Count to 10*. Holt, 1964.

Francoise. *Jeanne-Marie Counts Her Sheep*. Scribner, 1951.

Freschet, Berniece. *Where's Henrietta's Hen?* Il. by Lorinda Bryan Cauley. Putnam, 1980.

Friskey, Margaret. *Chicken Little, Count to Ten*. Children's Press, 1946.

Ginsburg, Mirra. *Kitten From One to Ten*. Il. by Giulio Maestro. Crown, 1980.

Gregor, Arthur. *1 2 3 4 5*. Lippincott, 1956.

Gretz, Susanne. *Teddy Bears 1 to 10*. Follett, 1969.

Hawkinson, Lucy. *Picture Book Farm*. Children's Press, 1971.

Hefter, Richard. *One White Crocodile Smile*. Strawberry Books, 1974.

Hefter, Richard and Martin Moskof. *Everything*. Parent's, 1971.

Hoban, Russell. *Ten What?* Scribner, 1974.

Hoban, Tana. *Count and See*. Collier, 1972.

Hutchins, Pat. *1 Hunter*. Greenwillow, 1982.

Ipcar, Dahlov. *Brown Cow Farm*. Doubleday, 1959.

Jackson, Shirley. *Nine Magic Wishes*. Crowell-Collier, 1963.

Jacobs, Leland, (ed.). *Delight in Number*. Holt, 1964.

Keats, Ezra Jack. *Over in the Meadow*. Four Winds, 1971.

Kredenzer, Gail and Stanley Mack. *One Dancing Drum*. S.G. Phillips, 1971.

Kruss, J. *3 x 3 Three by Three*. Macmillan, 1963.

Langstaff, John. *Over in the Meadow*. Il. by Feodor Rojankovsky. Harcourt, 1957.

LeSieg, Theo B. *Ten Apples Up On Top*. Random House, 1961.

Lewin, Betsy. *Cat Count*. Dodd, 1981.

Livermore, E. *One to Ten, Count Again*. Houghton Mifflin, 1973.

Lofgren, Uef. *One-Two-Three*. Addison-Wesley, 1974.

Mack, Stanley. *10 Bears In My Bed*. Pantheon, 1974.

Martin, Bill. *Ten Little Caterpillars*. Little, Brown, 1961.

Mathews, Louise. *Cluck One*. Il. by Jeni Bassett. Dodd, 1982.

McDonald, J. *Counting on an Elephant*. Puffin Penguin, 1976.

McLeod, Emilie. *One Snail and Me*. Il. by Walter Lorraine. Little, Brown, 1981.

Meeks, Esther. *One is the Engine*. Follett, 1972.

Mendoza, George. *The Marcel Marceau Counting Book*. Doubleday, 1971.

Merriam, Eve. *Project 1-2-3*. McGraw-Hill, 1971.

Merrill, Jean. *How Many Kids Are Hiding on My Block?* Whitman, 1970.

Milne, A.A. *Pooh's Counting Book*. Il. by E.H. Shepard. Dutton, 1982.

Montgomerie, Norah. *One, Two, Three*. Abelard-Schuman, 1967.

Nohelty, Sally, (Ed.). *Eleven and Three are Poetry*. Holt, 1964.

Nolan, Dennis. *Monster Bubbles*. Prentice-Hall, 1976.

Pavey, Pater. *One Dragon's Dream*. Bradbury, 1979.

Peppe, Rodney. *Circus Numbers*. Delacorte, 1969.

Reiss, John. *Numbers*. Bradbury, 1971.

Russell, Sandra Joanne. *A Farmer's Dozen*. Harper & Row, 1982.

Seiden, Art. *1 2 3 Board Book*. Grosset and Dunlap, 1948.

Sendak, Maurice. *One Was Johnny*. Harper & Row, 1962.

_____. *Seven Little Monsters*. Harper & Row, 1977.

Seymour, Brenda. *First Counting*. Walck, 1969.

Simon, Leonard. *Counting Lightly*. Walck, 1964.

Smith, D. *Farm Numbers*. Abelard-Schuman, 1970.

Thompson, Susan L. *One More Thing, Dad*. Il. by Dora Leder. Whitman, 1980.

True, Louise. *Number Men*. Children's Press, 1962.

Tudor, Tasha. *1 Is One*. Walck, 1956.

Wells, Rosemary. *Max's Toys, A Counting Book*. Dial, 1979.

Wildsmith, Brian. *Brian Wildsmith's 1, 2, 3's*. Watts, 1965.

Yolen, Jane. *An Invitation to the Butterfly Ball*. Parent's, 1976.

Alphabet Books

"All Butterflies"

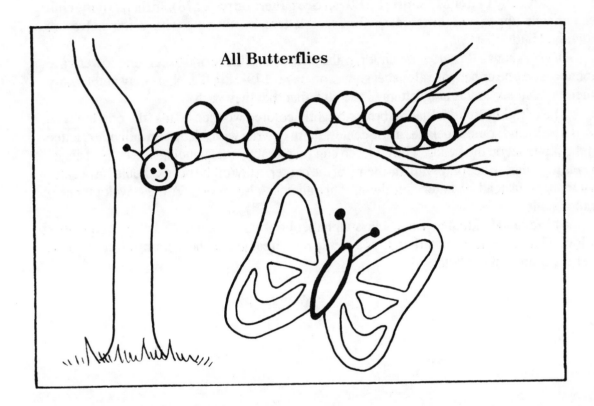

All Butterflies

The backdrop of the "All Butterflies" center (title taken from the book by Marcia Brown) is the bulletin board shown above. The caterpillar can be made from a variety of materials. Cloth or felt circles for the body will provide texture, or a fuzzy fabric will add a three-dimensional effect. The caterpillar may also be made from poster board. The butterfly can be made from any type of paper. The wings should be attached to the bulletin board only at the body with the outer edges free for a three-dimensional effect.

A table is needed in the center for the display of activities for the children.

1) **Butterfly Puzzle.** The purpose of this activity is to match capital and lower case alphabet letters. Cut *two* butterflies using the pattern on the page 177. Label the puzzle pieces on the first butterfly as shown, mixing upper case and lower case letters. On the second butterfly, write in each letter's upper/lower case counterpart in the corresponding puzzle piece. Cut one of the butterflies apart into puzzle pieces; leave the other one whole. When finished, the capital letters on the whole butterfly should be lower case letters on the puzzle pieces and the lower case letters on the whole butterfly should be capital letters on the puzzle pieces. The children then work the puzzle by matching the puzzle piece letter to its corresponding form on the whole butterfly.

2) **Alphabet Sequence Caterpillars.** (See pattern on page 178). Place five or six circles with sequential letters and a caterpillar head in individual envelopes. Children then arrange the letters in alphabetical order and make a caterpillar. This activity allows the children to work with sequences in the middle and end of the alphabet, instead of habitually beginning with *a*.

3) **Butterfly Letter Matching Puzzles.** (See pattern on page 178). In this activity, children match upper and lower case forms of letters by fitting together the halves of individual butterflies.

4) **Worksheet.** Provide the children the two caterpillar worksheets, one lower case alphabet and one upper case alphabet shown on pages 179-180. Teachers may include any other worksheets concerning letters of the alphabet that they wish.

5) **Stringing Beads.** Place a box of brightly colored wooden beads (the one-inch size works well) and some shoelaces in the center. Paint or write with felt tip pen individual letters of the alphabet on the beads. The children can then practice sequencing letters by stringing beads together. In keeping with the theme of the center, a few of the beads should have caterpillar faces instead of letters on them. This activity also assists in the development of motor skills.

6) Make individual or whole class alphabet books using some of the materials listed below. The use of these materials adds a tactile reinforcement to the learning of letter names and the shapes of the letters.

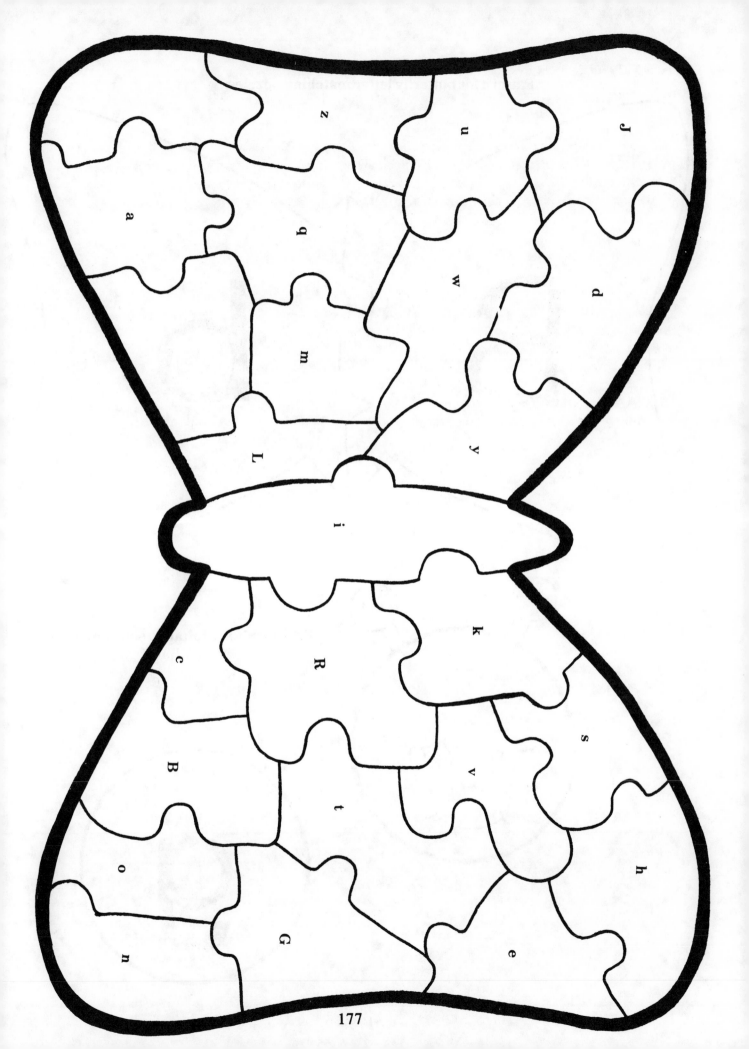

Pattern for butterfly letter matching puzzles:

Pattern for alphabet sequence caterpillars

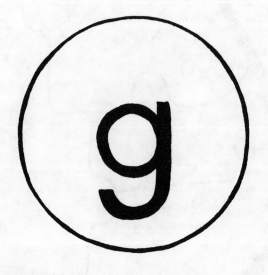

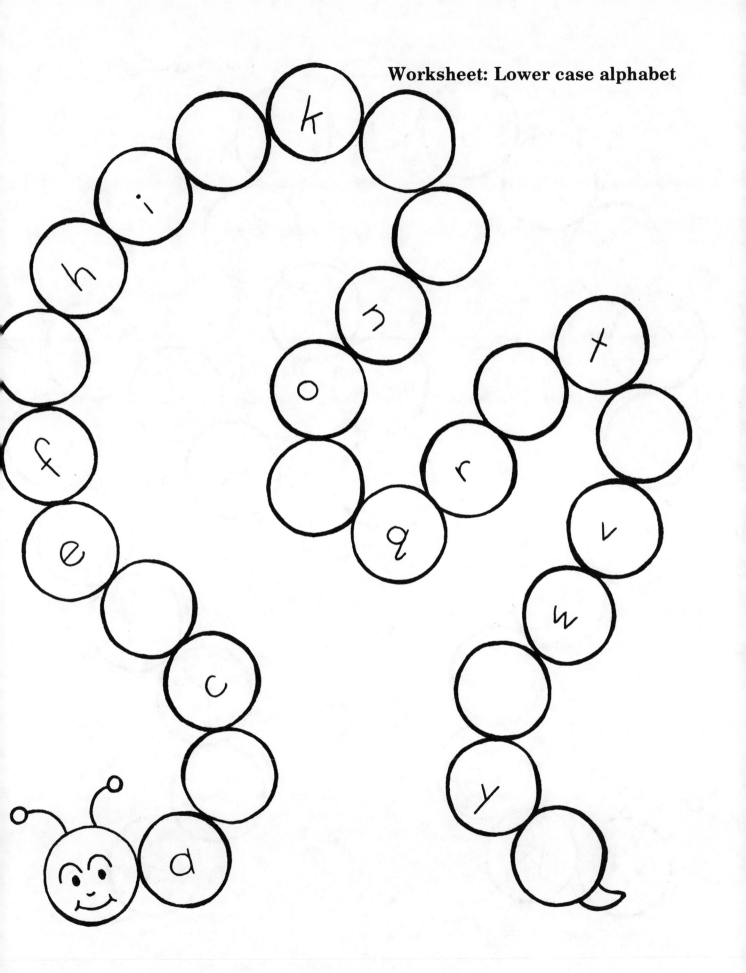

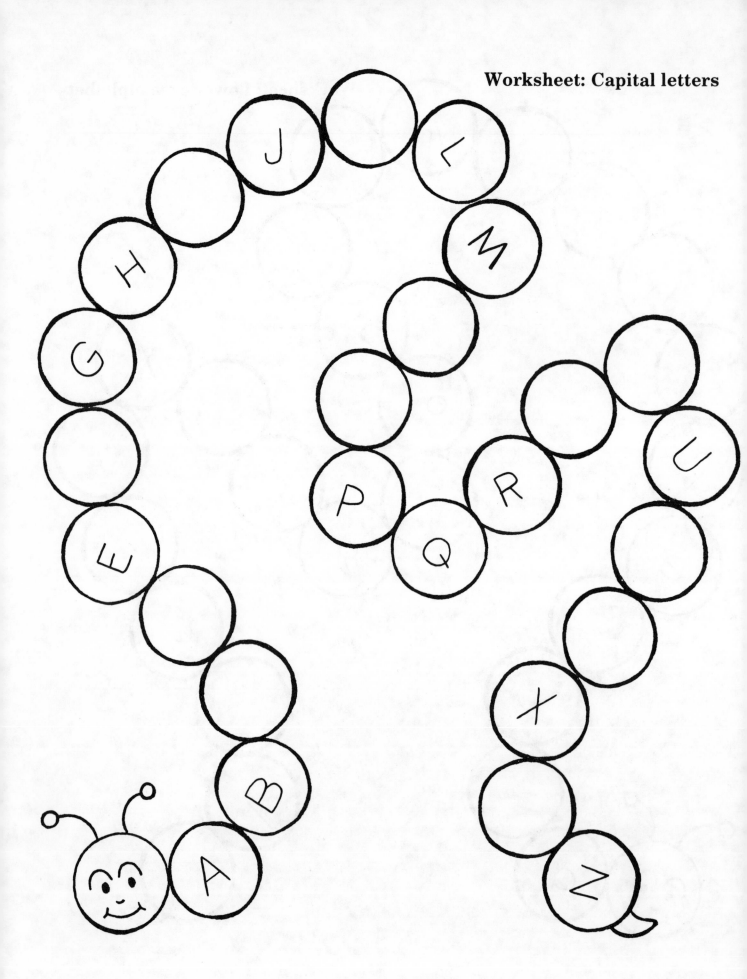

Suggested materials for the alphabet books: *

a alphabet macaroni
b beans
c corn (unpopped popcorn)
e eggshells (crushed)
f feathers, felt
g glitter
h hearts (cinnamon red "hots")
i ink
j jelly beans (miniature)
l lemon drops, leaves
m macaroni
n noodles
o oats
p peas

q quilts (pieces of different cloth, or wrapping paper with patch-work pattern)
r ribbon, rice
s sunflower seeds, sandpaper
t twigs, toothpicks
v Valentine candy hearts (small hearts with sayings)
w wood (for example, popsicle sticks, tongue depressors, twigs)
x almost anything goes
y yarn
z ric rac trim (because it zig-zags)

*Teachers may substitute other appropriate materials for those listed above.

SELECTED BIBLIOGRAPHY OF ALPHABET BOOKS

Anno, Mitsumasa. *Anno's Alphabet*. Crowell, 1975.

Azarian, Mary. *A Farmer's Alphabet*. Godine, 1981.

Barton, Byron. *Applebet Story*. Viking, 1972.

Baskin, Leonard. *Hosie's Alphabet*. Viking, 1972.

Berger, Terry. *Ben's ABC Day*. Photographs by Alice Kandell. Lothrop, 1982.

Brown, Marcia. *All Butterflies*. Scribner, 1974.

_____. *Peter Piper's Alphabet*. Scribner, 1959.

Bruna, Dick. *B is For Bear; An ABC*. Methuen, 1971.

Burningham, John. *ABCDEFGHIJKLMNOPQRSTUVWXYZ*. Bobbs-Merrill, 1964.

Carle, Eric. *All About Arthur*. Watts, 1974.

Chardiet, Bernice. *C is For Circus*. Walker, 1971.

Charles, Donald. *Letters from the Calico Cat*. Children's Press, 1974.

_____. *Shaggy Dog's Animal Alphabet*. Children's Press, 1979.

Chess, Victoria. *Alfred's Alphabet Walk*. Greenwillow, 1979.

Chwast, Seymour and Martin Moskof. *Still Another Alphabet Book*. McGraw-Hill, 1969.

Cooney, Barbara. *A Garland of Games and Other Diversions; An Alphabet Book*. Holt, 1969.

Crowther, Robert. *The Most Amazing Hide-and-Seek Alphabet Book*. Viking, 1977.

Delauney, Sonia. *Alphabet*. Crowell, 1972.

Duvoisin, Roger. *A For The Ark*. Lothrop, 1952.

Eichenberg, Fritz. *Ape in a Cape*. Harcourt, 1952.

Emberley, Ed. *Ed Emberley's ABC*. Little, Brown, 1978.

Falls, C.B. *ABC*. Doubleday, 1923.

Farber, Norma. *I Found Them in the Yellow Pages*. Little, Brown, 1973.

_____. *This is the Ambulance Leaving the Zoo*. Dutton, 1975.

Feelings, Muriel. *Jambo Means Hello*. Il. by Tom Feelings. Dial, 1974.

Freeman, Don. *Add-a-Line Alphabet*. Golden Gate, 1968.

Fujikawa, Gyo. *A to Z Picture Book*. Grosset and Dunlap, 1974.

Gag, Wanda. *The ABC Bunny*. Coward-McCann, 1933.

Garten, Jan. *The Alphabet Tale*. Random House, 1964.

Gorey, Edward. *The Utter Zoo, an Alphabet*. Hawthorn, 1967.

Grant, Sandy. *Hey, Look at Me! A City ABC*. Bradbury, 1973.

Greenaway, Kate. *A Apple Pie*. Warne, n.d.

Gretz, Susanna. *Teddybears ABC*. Follett, 1975.

Grossbart, Francine. *A Big City*. Harper & Row, 1966.

Guthrie, Vee. *Animals From A to Z*. Van Nostrand, 1969.

Hoban, Tana. *A, B, See!* Greenwillow, 1982.

Hoberman, Mary Ann. *Nuts to You and Nuts to Me; An Alphabet of Poems*. Knopf, 1974.

Holl, Adelaide. *The ABC of Cars, Trucks, and Machines*. Heritage Press, 1970.

Hunter, Julius. *Absurd Alphabedtime Stories*. Bethany Press, 1976.

Hyman, Trina Schart. *A Little Alphabet*. Little, Brown, 1980.

Illsley, Velma. *M Is For Moving*. Walck, 1966.

Ipcar, Dahlov. *I Love My Anteater With an A*. Knopf, 1964.

Isadora, Rachel. *City Seen From A to Z*. Greenwillow, 1983.

Johnson, Crockett. *Harold's ABC*. Harper & Row, 1963.

King, Tony. *The Moving Alphabet*. Putnam, 1982.

Knight, Hilary. *Hilary Knight's ABC*. Golden Press, 1961.

Kraus, Robert. *Good Night Little ABC*. Springfellow Books, 1973.

Lionni, Leo. *The Alphabet Tree*. Pantheon, 1968.

Lobel, Arnold. *On Market Street*. Il. by Anita Lobel. Greenwillow, 1981.

Matthiesen, Thomas, *ABC and Alphabet Book*. Platt and Munk, 1966.

McGinley, Phyllis. *All Around the Town*. Lippincott, 1948.

Mendoza, George. *The Marcel Marceau Alphabet Book*. Doubleday, 1970.

Merriam, Eve. *Good Night to Annie*. Il. by John Wallner. Four Winds, 1980.

Miles, Miska. *Apricot ABC*. Little, Brown, 1969.

Miller, Barry. *Alphabet World*. Macmillan, 1971.

Milne, A.A. *Pooh's Alphabet Book*. Dutton, 1975.

Montressor, Beni. *A for Angel*. Knopf, 1969.

Munari, Bruno. *ABC*. World, 1960.

Niland, Deborah. *ABC of Monsters*. McGraw-Hill, 1976.

Oxenbury, Helen. *ABC of Things*. Watts, 1972.

Parish, Peggy. *A Beastly Circus*. Simon and Schuster, 1969.

Peppe, Rodney. *The Alphabet Book*. Four Winds, 1968.

Piatti, Celestino. *Animal ABC*. Atheneum, 1966.

Provenson, Alice and Martin. *A Peaceable Kingdom*. Viking, 1978.

Rey, H.A. *Curious George Learns the Alphabet*. Houghton Mifflin, 1963.

Rockwell, Anne. *Albert B. Cub and Zebra*. Crowell, 1977.

Rojankovsky, Feodor. *Animals in the Zoo*. Knopf, 1962.

Schmiderer, Dorothy. *The Alphabeast Book*. Holt, 1971.

Sedgwick, Paulita. *Circus ABC*. Holt, 1978.

Sendak, Maurice. *Alligators All Around*. Harper & Row, 1962.

Tallon, Robert. *Zoophabets*. Bobbs-Merrill, 1971.

_____. *Rotten Kidphabets*. Holt, 1975.

Tudor, Tasha. *A Is For Annabelle*. Walck, 1954.

Walters, Marguerite. *The City-Country ABC*. Doubleday, 1966.

Warburg, Sandol. *From Ambledee to Zumbledee*. Houghton Mifflin, 1968.

Waters, Frank. *The First ABC*. Watts, 1970.

Watson, Clyde. *Applebet*. Il. by Wendy Watson. Farrar, Straus and Giroux, 1982.

Wild, Robin and Jocelyn. *The Bears' ABC Book*. Lippincott, 1977.

Wildsmith, Brian. *ABC*. Watts, 1962.

Yolen, Jane. *All in the Woodland Early*. Il. by Jane Breskin Zalben. Collins, 1979.

Nursery Rhyme Books

The "Mary, Mary, quite contrary" activity bulletin board (shown on the next page) is the backdrop for the center. A table for the display of other activities and a cassette tape recorder are also needed. Directions for "Mary, Mary, quite contrary" bulletin board:

When making the bulletin board, glue or staple the flowers around the edges but leave the tops free so that each flower forms a "pocket." Have available picture cards with pictures of objects of different colors. These pictures can be taken from magazines, catalogs, coloring books, etc., and mounted on index cards. Place the cards in a plastic watering can and put the can in the center. Children are to draw cards from the can and place them in the correct flowers, according to the labeled color. This activity provides practice with discrimination of colors and exposure to color words. (The color labels on the flowers can be changed to letters, numerals, etc., and the cards can be changed accordingly.) Additional flowers may be included. Other activities:

1) For an art activity, ask the children: What does Mother Goose look like? Have them draw their various interpretations and display the pictures around the center.

2) As a creative dramatic activity, have the children act out nursery rhyme characters, such as Little Boy Blue, Little Miss Muffet, Jack Be Nimble, Jack and Jill, etc. While one or two children are acting, the remainder of the children can repeat the nursery rhyme.

3) Display a variety of Mother Goose books (see bibliography). Conduct small group discussions of how characters are portrayed differently by different illustrators.

Mary, Mary, quite contrary,
How does your garden grow?

purple

yellow

green

blue

red

184

4) To develop auditory discrimination and the concept of rhyming words, prepare the set of picture cards (simple drawings or cutouts from magazines, etc.) and a tape similar to the following:

"I want you to place all the picture cards face up on the table. (Pause to allow children to comply.)

Now, listen to this Mother Goose rhyme:

Little Boy Blue, come blow your horn,
The sheep's in the meadow, the cow's in the corn,
Where is the boy that looks after the sheep?
He's under the haystack fast asleep.

Find the picture of the *horn*. (Pause for a few seconds to allow the children to find the picture.) Now find a picture of something that sound like *horn*. (Pause) Did you find the picture of *corn*? Good. *Horn* sound like *corn*. *Horn* rhymes with *corn*."

Proceed on the tape with these nursery rhymes and picture cards:

"Hey Diddle Diddle" — moon, spoon
"Georgie Porgy" — pie, cry
"Mary, Mary, Quite Contrary" — bells, shells
"Old Woman Who Lived in a Shoe" — bread, bed
"Crooked Little Man" — mouse, house

Other nursery rhymes may be substituted for these suggestions.

5) Place "Peter's Pumpkin Shell" activity in the center (see page 186). Place "Buckle My Shoe" sequencing activity in the center (see page 187.)

6) Have children make "Humpty Dumpty" puzzles.

Directions for "Peter's Pumpkin Shell" Activity:

Based on the nursery rhyme "Peter, Peter, Pumpkin Eater," this activity requires children to match pictured objects with the letters representing their beginning consonant sounds. The activity board is a large chart in the shape of a pumpkin. Small pockets labeled with different consonant letters are attached to the pumpkin chart. A large pocket in the center of the chart contains the picture cards. Pictures may be cut from old workbooks, catalogs, coloring books, etc., and mounted on index cards. Children are to place the pictures in the pockets with the corresponding initial consonants. There should be more than one picture card for each consonant. Consonant labels should not be permanently attached so that letters and pictures can be changed periodically. Pictures that begin with consonant blends and digraphs (such as "flag" and "shoe") should be avoided.

The pumpkin can be made from poster board or cardboard. Library pockets that hold cards in the backs of library books may be used for the small pockets on the pumpkin. A large brown mailing envelope will work well for holding the picture cards.

This activity can be modified to provide practice with ending consonants, blends, digraphs, and vowel sounds.

Model of "Peter's Pumpkin Shell"

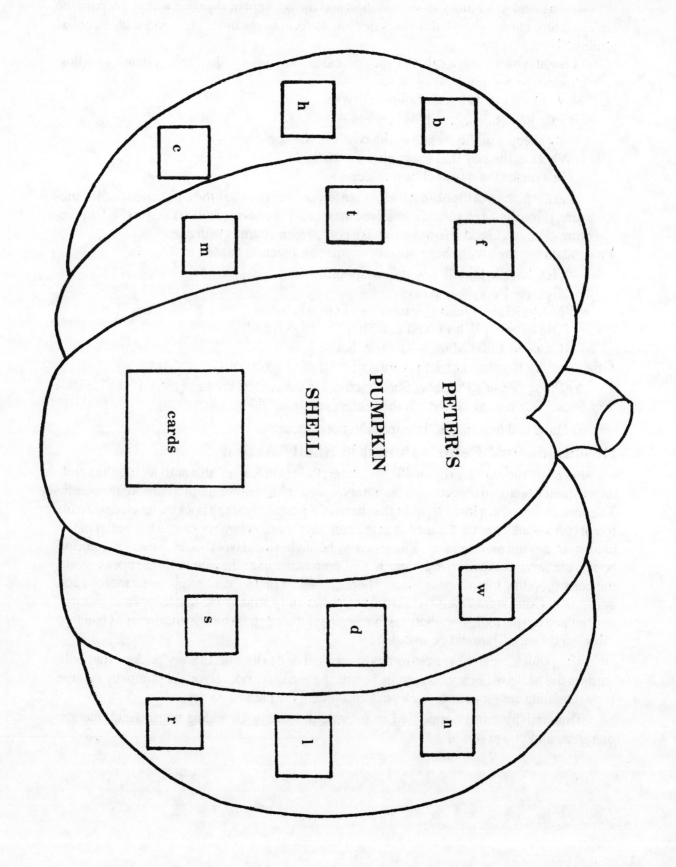

"One, Two, Buckle My Shoe" Sequencing Activity:

The rhyme may be shared with the children orally or may be recorded on tape for the children to listen to. Children may place the cards in the correct sequence on a table or along a chalkboard ledge. The following numeral cards will need to be added to the cards below: 1, 2, 3, 4, 5, 6, 7, 8, 9, 10.

(actual card size)

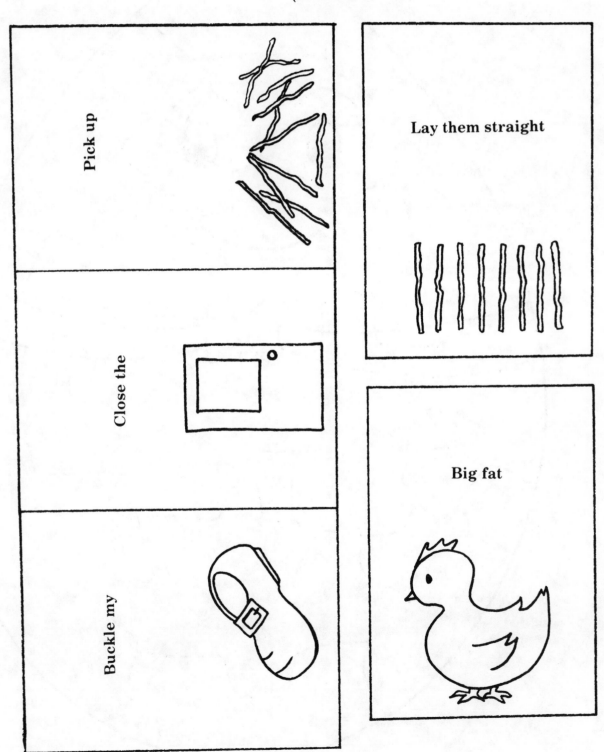

Humpty Dumpty Puzzle

Give each child a ditto of the puzzle to color. Have the children color the picture and then mount the puzzle on posterboard, cut around the outside, and cut along the dotted lines. Each then has a puzzle to take home and can literally put "Humpty Dumpty back together again" many times.

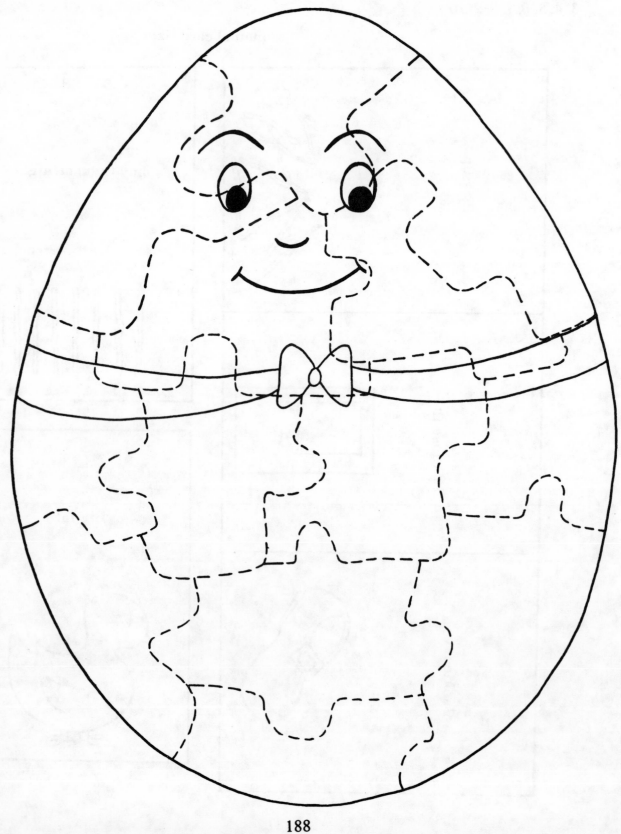

188

SELECTED BIBLIOGRAPHY OF NURSERY RHYME BOOKS

Alderson, Brian. *Cakes and Custard*. Morrow, 1975

Anglund, Joan Walsh. *In A Pumpkin Shell*. Harcourt, 1960.

Bayley, Nicola. *Nicola Bayley's Book of Nursery Rhymes*. Knopf, 1975.

Bodecker, N.M. *It's Raining, Said John Twaining*. Atheneum, 1973.

Briggs, Raymond. *The White Land*. Coward,-McCann, 1963.

_____. *The Mother Goose Treasury*. Coward-McCann, 1966.

Brooke, Leslie. *Ring O' Roses*. Warne, 1923.

Chorao, Kay. *The Baby's Lap Book*. Dutton, 1977.

Cranston, Margaret. *1, 2, Buckle My Shoe*. Holt, 1967.

de Angeli, Marguerite. *Book of Mother Goose and Nursery Rhymes*. Doubleday, 1952.

Emberly, Ed. *London Bridge is Falling Down*. Little, Brown, 1967.

Fish, Helen Dean. *Four and Twenty Blackbirds*. Lippincott, 1965.

Frasconi, Antonio. *The House That Jack Built*. Harcourt, 1958.

Fujikawa, Gyo. *Mother Goose*. Grosset and Dunlap, 1968.

Galdone, Paul. *The Old Woman and Her Pig*. McGraw-Hill, 1960.

_____. *Old Mother Hubbard and Her Dog*. McGraw-Hill, 1960.

_____. *The House That Jack Built*. McGraw-Hill, 1961.

_____. *Tom, Tom, The Piper's Son*. McGraw-Hill, 1964.

_____. *The History of Simple Simon*. McGraw-Hill, 1966.

Greenaway, Kate. *Mother Goose, or The Old Nursery Rhymes*. Warne, n.d.

Hogrogrian, Nonny. *One is Love, Two is Love, and Other Loving Mother Goose Rhymes*. Dutton, 1972.

Jeffers, Susan. *Three Jovial Huntsmen*. Bradbury, 1973.

_____. *If Wishes Were Horses and Other Rhymes*. Dutton, 1979.

Kent, Jack. *Merry Mother Goose*. Golden Press, 1977.

Lines, Kathleen. *Lavender's Blue*. Watts, 1954.

Lobel, Arnold. *Gregory Griggs and Other Nursery Rhyme People*. Greenwillow, 1978.

Marshall, James. *James Marshall's Mother Goose*. Farrar, Straus, and Giroux, 1979.

Mitchell, Donald. *Every Child's Book of Nursery Songs*. Bonanza Books, 1969.

Ness, Evaline. *Old Mother Hubbard*. Holt, 1972.

Parsons, Virginia. *Animal Parade· Mother Goose Rhymes*. Doubleday, 1970.

Petersham, Maud and Miska. *The Rooster Crows*. Macmillan, 1945.

Potter, Beatrix. *Appley Dapply's Nursery Rhymes*. Warne, 1917.

Provenson, Alice and Martin. *The Mother Goose Book*. Random, 1976.

Rackham, Arthur. *Mother Goose, Old Nursey Rhymes*. Appleton, 1913.

Reed, Philip. *Mother Goose and Nursery Rhymes*. Atheneum, 1963.

Richardson, Frederick. *Mother Goose*. Hubbard, 1962.

Rockwell, Anne. *Gray Goose and Gander and Other Mother Goose Rhymes*. Crowell, 1980.

Rojankovsky, Feodor. *The Tall Book of Mother Goose*. Harper & Row, 1942.

Seward, Prudence. *The First Book of Nursery Rhymes*. Watts, 1970.

Spier, Peter. *And So My Garden Grows*. Doubleday, 1967.

_____. *To Market, To Market*. Doubleday, 1967.

_____. *London Bridge Is Falling Down*. Doubleday, 1967.

Torrey, Marjorie. *Sing Mother Goose*. Dutton, 1945.

Tripp, Wallace. *Granfa' Grig Had a Pig*. Little, Brown, 1976.

Tucker, Nicholas. *Mother Goose Abroad*. Crowell, 1974.

Tudor, Tasha. *Mother Goose*. Walck, 1944.

Watson, Clyde. *Father Fox's Pennyrhymes*. Crowell, 1971.

Weil, Lisl. *Mother Goose Picture Riddles· A Book of Rebuses*. Holiday, 1981.

Wheeler, Opal. *Sing Mother Goose*. Dutton, 1945.

Wildsmith, Brian. *Brian Wildsmith's Mother Goose*. Watts, 1965.

Wright, Blanche Fisher. *The Real Mother Goose*. Rand McNally, 1965.

CHAPTER NINE

Wordless Books

Wordless books are picture books in which the story is told entirely through pictures. The action and sequence must be clearly depicted, as there are no words to explain the picture or to effect transition from one scene to the next.

Wordless books are a relatively recent addition to the field of children's literature. Books of this type are particulary valuable when used in the development of oral language skills, as a stimulus in the language experience approach, as an aid in developing book handling skills and front-to-back and left-to-right progression, and in the development of the concept of sequencing.

Wordless books are available in a wide range of difficulty levels as reflected in the amount of detail depicted and plot complexity. Although there are no words to interfere with "reading" these books, one must consider the conceptual as well as the interest levels of the children for whom the books are being selected. A bibliography of wordless books concludes this chapter.

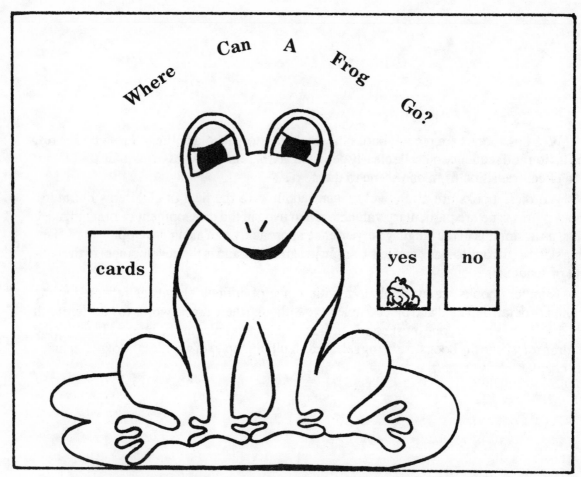

Display along with this bulletin board the series of books by Mercer Mayer: *A Boy, A Dog, and A Frog; Frog, Where Are You?; A Boy, A Dog, A Frog, and A Friend; Frog Goes to Dinner; Frog On His Own; One Frog Too Many.*

Directions for playing: The children are to sort the phrase cards into the "Yes" and "No" pockets. The correct phrase cards, indicating places where real frogs would go, are coded on the back with a picture of a frog. (This activity may tie in with a science lesson of frogs.)

Suggested phrases:

YES	NO
in the lake	in a cake
in a pond	in a fly
to the beach	on a top
by the water	near the wash
on the sand	on a ball
for a swim	on a swing
on the rocks	to school
in the mud	to the store

Compound Word Game

Read *Alligator's Toothache* by Diane deGroat.
    Shrewbettina's Birthday by John Goodall.
Directions for playing:

The object of the game is for children to go from 'Start" to the "Birthday Party" by matching the parts of the compound words. Since there are many delicious things to eat pictured in the books, all the compound words are names of foods. Two to four children may play. Players roll a die to see who goes first. A homemade die is suggested for this game. (A square of sponge makes a good die — it rolls quietly.) Put one, two or three dots on the faces of the die so that the highest number the players may roll is "3".

The game calls for a deck of *A* cards and a deck of *B* cards. Each *A* and *B* card contains a part of a compound word. In addition, several "Dentist" cards must be scattered at random throughout both decks. Each player in turn draws an *A* and *B* card in an attempt to make a compound word. If a match is made, the player lays the matched pair down on the table and rolls the die to see how many spaces he/she may move. If no match is made, the player discards the *B* card. The players keep all *A* cards until matches are made. The player must pronounce both words of every pair of cards drawn. When *B* cards are gone, the discard pile becomes the *B* pile.

As players move around the board, they may land on a "toothache" space. When that happens, players proceed directly to the "Dentist" along the path. A player may leave the "Dentist" by drawing a "Dentist" card from either deck. When he/she draws a "Dentist" card, the player returns to the original spot but gets no attempt at a match on that turn. Play until all children have reached the party. (A party isn't much fun unless everyone is there.)

List of compound words that may be used:

cupcake	potato chip	blackberry
pancake	blueberry	applesauce
ice cream	hot dog	grapefruit
peanuts	green beans	strawberry
popcorn	cornbread	jelly beans
pineapple	milkshake	chocolate chip
watermelon	eggrolls	French fries
mushroom	meatballs	peppermint

SAMPLE GAME CARDS

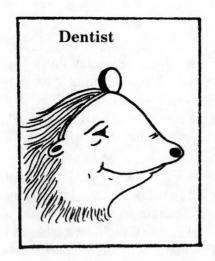

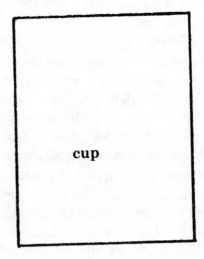

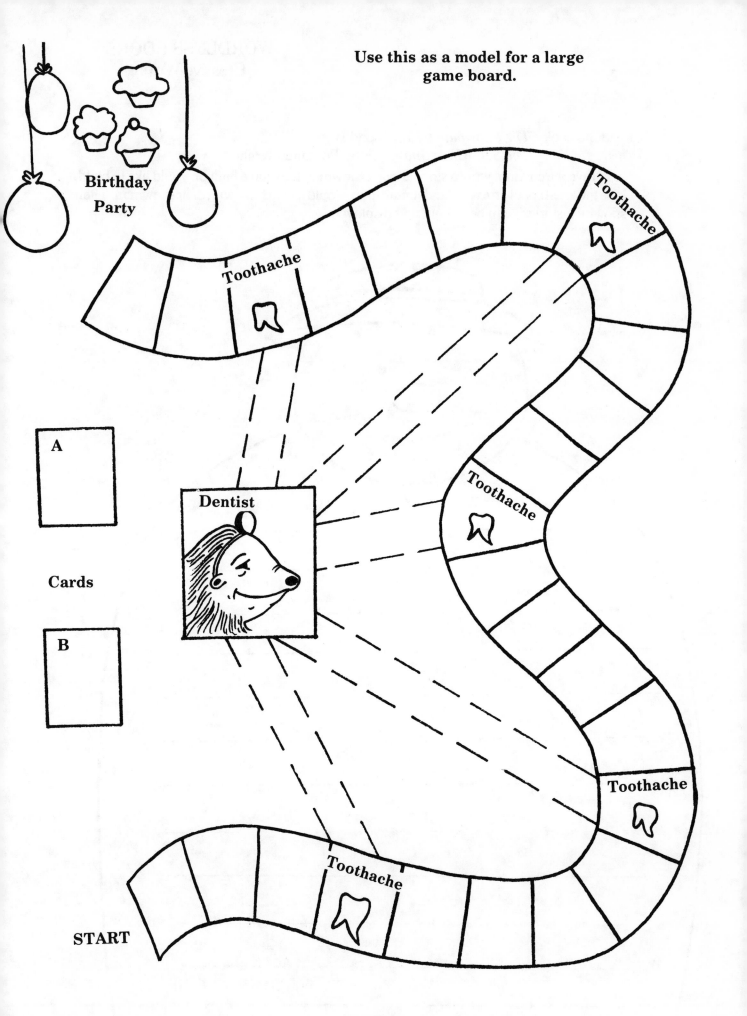

Use this as a model for a large game board.

Birthday Party

Toothache

Toothache

Toothache

A

Cards

B

Dentist

Toothache

Toothache

START

197

Read the books: *The Snowman* by Raymond Briggs
The Self-Made Snowman by Fernando Krahn

Have the children write a story about a snowman they have built or would like to build. Have them tell about an exciting adventure they would like to have with their snowman. Their "snowmen stories" can be cut out and displayed.

198

Read *Bubble Bubble* by Mercer Mayer.
Write words in the bubbles.

Things that are soft.

Things that are light.

Write a story using some of your words.

_____

_____

_____

_____

_____

_____

_____

_____

_____

_____

_____

_____

Things that can fly.

Read *Bobo's Dream* by Martha Alexander.

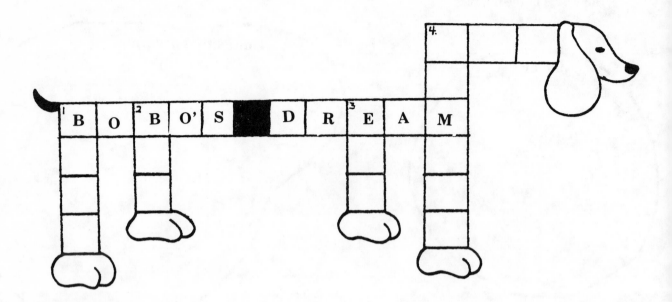

Directions: Read the sentences below. Write a word in the space that will fit the meaning of the sentence. Use letter clues from the puzzle to help. Then write the words in the puzzle.

Note: This page may be duplicated, or it may be placed on tagboard and laminated so that children can write on it and wipe it off.

DOWN
1. The boy in the story read a _____.
2. Opposite of girl. _____
3. You _____ your food.
4. Sounds like jumped. _____
ACROSS
4. A mouse is little, but an elephant is ____

Read: *How Santa Had a Long and Difficult Journey Delivering His Presents* by
Fernando Krahn.

Directions: Make up clues for this puzzle for a friend to do.

1.

2.

3.

4.

5.

6.

Read *Elephant Buttons* by Noriko Ueno.

Make a cloth elephant (see pattern on page 205) to hold a set of cards depicting the animals in the book (see next page for sample cards). Children are to place the cards in the same sequence as the animals appear in the story. Children may need to refer to the book in their first experiences with this activity. Number the animal cards on the back for self-checking. For children who are ready for words, the names of the animals may be placed on the cards instead of the pictures.

A poster board elephant may be used instead of a cloth one for this activity. An envelope containing the cards may be attached to the back of the cut-out elephant.

Sequence cards for ELEPHANT BUTTONS:

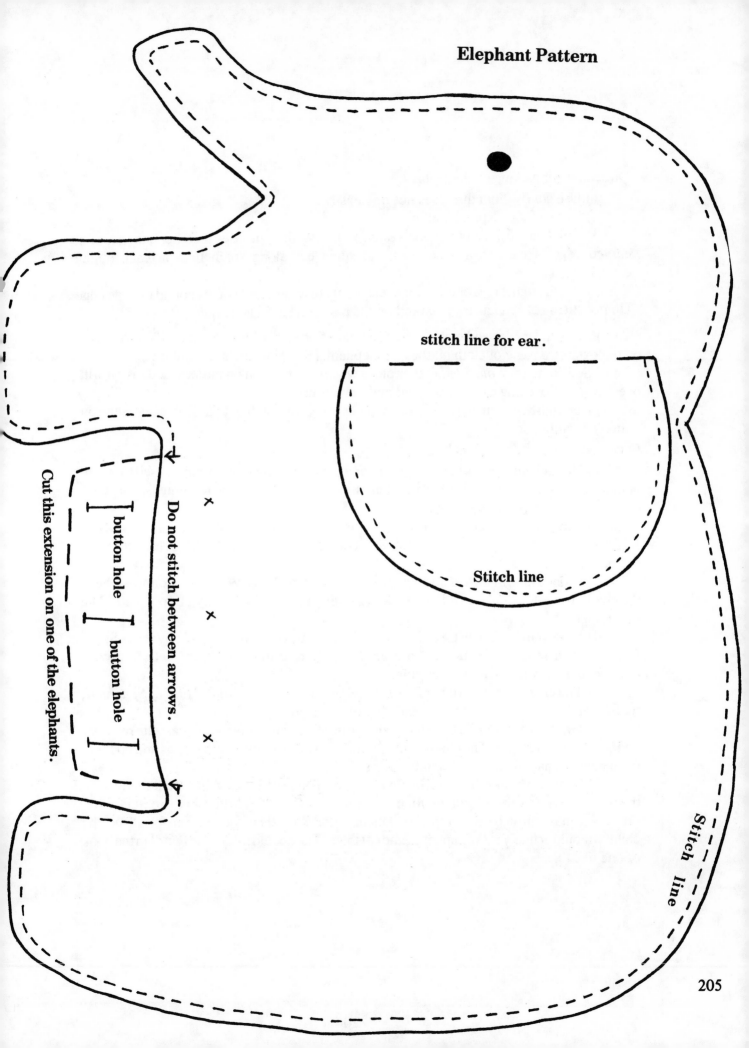

Elephant Pattern

stitch line for ear.

Stitch line

Do not stitch between arrows.

button hole

button hole

Cut this extension on one of the elephants.

Stitch line

205

Directions for making cloth elephant:

1) Use sturdy cloth that does not fray easily.

2) Cut *2* of the elephant patterns.

3) Cut *4* ears from cloth of contrasting color. With right sides together, stitch around curved edge of ear. Turn inside out and stitch ear along stitch line on each outline elephant.

4) Put the right sides of the outline elephants together, and stitch around outside edge. Do not stitch between arrows marked on the pattern. Turn inside out.

5) Turn under edge and make 2 or 3 (depending on size of buttons desired) buttonholes on the extended piece of cloth on the one elephant. (See placement on pattern.)

6) Sew buttons on *outside* of other piece where *x* is marked on pattern. Extension will overlap so the opening can be buttoned and unbuttoned.

7) For finishing touches, sew on a piece of yarn for the tail. For eyes, sew on buttons or embroider.

Other activities with wordless books:

1) Have children work in small groups and collect pictures which can be used to create books based on *Look Again* by Tana Hoban. Place finished books in the center so that children may enjoy those done by other groups.

2) Have the children write ringmaster introductions for each of the acts in *Brian Wildsmith's Circus* by Brian Wildsmith. The children may want to select some to dramatize.

3) Using *The Good Bird* and *The Naughty Bird*, by Peter Wezel, as examples, have the children create parallel wordless books. (For example, "The Happy Hippo" and "The Sad Hippo.")

4) Have the children list some of the animals pictured in *Noah's Ark*, by Peter Spier, and classify them as to type, such as "farm animals," "jungle animals," "pets," etc. Many different classification groups are possible.

5) The children may write or illustrate sequels to *A Flying Saucer Full of Spaghetti*, by Fernando Krahn, in which they tell what the little elves will do next.

6) Have several wordless books available in a listening center with a cassette recorder and blank cassette tapes. The children may tell stories on tape and put the tapes and books in the center so that others may listen to their stories.

7) Share the book *Pancakes for Breakfast* by Tomie de Paola with the children. Have them list in sequence the ingredients for making pancakes that the old lady had to obtain. Children could make up their own recipes for pancakes and share them for fun. As a follow-up, the children could actually make pancakes and eat them. They could follow the recipe in the book or one like this:

PANCAKES

1 egg   1 T. sugar
1 cup flour   3 t. baking powder
¾ cup milk   2 T. shortening, melted, or vegetable oil
½ t. salt

Beat egg with hand beater until fluffy; beat in remaining ingredients until smooth. For thinner pancakes, stir in additional ¼ cup milk. Grease heated griddle if necessary. Pour about 3 tablespoons batter onto griddle per pancake. Cook pancakes until puffed and dry around edges. Turn and cook other sides until golden brown. Makes about nine 4-inch pancakes.

8) Using pieces of construction paper in different colors, have the children create objects similar to what the little wooden man and women make in *Changes, Changes* by Pat Hutchins. All their pictures could be put together to make a class "Changes, Changes" book.

9) Children can create short picture stories similar to those in *Flicks* by Tomie de Paola. These can be put on special filmstrip film, and children can view them as if they were at the movies. Instead of a filmstrip, the pictures could be drawn on large Baggies with felt tip pens. The Baggies are then arranged in order and fastened together with masking tape. The stories can be shown on an overhead projector. Lower the lights, pop some corn, and enjoy the "flicks."

10) A comparison of the book *Deep in the Forest* by Brinton Turkle and a version of "The Three Bears" can serve as the springboard for an oral discussion activity.

SELECTED BIBLIOGRAPHY OF WORDLESS BOOKS

Alexander, Martha. *Bobo's Dream*. Dial, 1970.

_____. *Out! Out! Out!* Dial, 1970.

Amoss, Bertha. *By The Sea*. Parent's, 1969.

Anderson, Laurie. *The Package*. Bobbs-Merrill, 1971.

Anno, Mitsumasa. *Anno's Alphabet*. Crowell, 1975.

_____. *Anno's Counting Book*. Crowell, 1975.

_____. *Anno's Journey*. Collins World, 1977.

_____. *Anno's Animals*. Collins World, 1979.

Ardizzone, Edward. *The Wrong Side of the Bed*. Doubleday, 1970.

Aruego, Jose. *Look What I Can Do*. Scribner, 1971.

Asch, Frank. *The Blue Balloon*. McGraw-Hill, 1971.

_____. *In the Eye of the Teddy*. Harper & Row, 1973.

Bang, Molly. *The Grey Lady and the Strawberry Snatcher*. Four Winds, 1980.

Barton, Byron. *Elephant*. Seabury, 1971.

_____. *The Elephant's Visit*. Little, Brown, 1975.

Baum, Willi. *Birds of a Feather*. Addison-Wesley, 1969.

Bird, Malcolm. *The Sticky Child*. Harcourt, 1981.

Bolliger-Savelli, Antonella. *The Knitted Cat*. Macmillan, 1972.

Briggs, Raymond. *The Snowman*. Random House, 1978.

Brinckloe. *The Spider Web*. Doubleday, 1974.

Carle, Eric. *Do You Want to be My Friend?* Crowell, 1971.

_____. *Have You Seen My Cat?* Watts, 1973.

_____. *I See a Song*. Crowell, 1973.

_____. *A Very Long Tail*. Crowell, 1972.

_____. *A Very Long Train*. Crowell, 1972.

Carrick, Donald. *Drip Drop*. Macmillan, 1973.

Carroll, Ruth. *The Chimp and the Clown*. Walck, 1968.

_____. *The Christmas Kitten*. Walck, 1970.

_____. *The Dolphin and the Mermaid*. Walck, 1974.

_____. *Rolling Down Hill*. Walck, 1973.

_____. *What Whisker Did*. Walck, 1965.

Charlot, Martha. *Sunnyside Up*. Weatherhill, 1972.

Crews, Donald. *Truck*. Greenwillow, 1980.

de Groat, Diane. *Alligator's Toothache*. Crown, 1977.

de Paola, Tomie. *Pancakes for Breakfast*. Harcourt, 1978.

_____. *Flick*. Harcourt, 1979.

Emberley, Ed. *A Birthday Wish*. Little, Brown, 1977.

Espenschied, Gertrude, *Oh Ball*. Harper &Row, 1966.

Fromm, Lilo. *Muffel and Plums*. Macmillan, 1972.

Fuchs, Eric. *Journey to the Moon*. Delacorte, 1969.

Gilbert, Elliot. *A Cat*. Holt, 1963.

Giovannetti. *Max*. Atheneum, 1977.

Goodall, John. *The Adventures of Paddy Pork*. Harcourt, 1968.

_____. *The Ballooning Adventures of Paddy Pork*. Harcourt, 1969.

_____. *Paddy's Evening Out*. Atheneum, 1973.

_____. *Paddy Pork's Holiday*. Atheneum, 1976.

_____. *Paddy's New Hat*. Atheneum, 1980.

_____. *Paddy Goes Traveling*. Atheneum, 1982.

_____. *Paddy Finds a Job· A Pop-Up Story*. Atheneum, 1981.

_____. *Creepy Castle*. Atheneum, 1975.

_____. *Jacko*. Harcourt, 1972.

_____. *The Midnight Adventures of Kelly, Dot and Esmerelda*. Atheneum, 1972.

_____. *Naughty Nancy*. Atheneum, 1975.

_____. *Shrewbettina's Birthday*. Harcourt, 1971.

_____. *The Surprise Picnic*. Atheneum, 1977.

_____. *Shrewbettina Goes to Work· A Pop-Up Story*. Atheneum, 1981.

Goshorn, Elizabeth. *Shoestrings*. Carolrhoda Books, 1975.

Hamberger, John. *The Lazy Dog*. Four Winds, 1971.

_____. *The Sleepless Day*. Four Winds , 1973.

Hartelius, Margaret. *The Chicken's Child*. Doubleday, 1975.

Hauptmann, Tatjana. *A Day in the Life of Petronella Pig*. Holt, 1982.

Hoban, Tana. *Circles, Triangles and Squares*. Macmillan, 1974.

_____. *Is It Red? Is It Yellow? Is It Blue?* Greenwillow, 1978.

_____. *Look Again!* Macmillan, 1971.

_____. *Over, Under and Through*. Macmillan, 1973.

_____. *Push Pull, Empty, Full*. Macmillan, 1972.

_____. *Shapes and Things*. Macmillan, 1970.

_____. *Take Another Look*. Greenwillow, 1981.

Hoest, William, *A Taste of Carrot*. Atheneum, 1967.

Hogrogian, Nonny *Apples*. Macmillan, 1972.

Hughes, Shirley. *Up and Up*. Prentice-Hall, 1979.

Hutchins, Pat. *Changes, Changes*. Macmillan, 1971.

Keats, Ezra Jack. *Kitten for a Day*. Four Winds, 1982.

_____. *Psst! Doggie*. Watts, 1973.

_____. *Skates*. Watts, 1973.

_____. *Clementina's Cactus*. Viking, 1982.

Kent, Jack. *The Egg Book*. Macmillan, 1975.

_____. *The Scribble Monster*. Harcourt, 1981.

Krahn, Fernando. *The Biggest Christmas Tree on Earth*. Atlantic, Little, 1978.

_____. *The Flying Saucer Full of Spaghetti*. Dutton, 1970.

_____. *The Self-Made Snowman*. Lippincott, 1974.

_____. *How Santa Claus Had a Long and Difficult Journey Delivering His Presents*. Delacorte, 1970.

_____. *Robot-Bot-Bot*. Dutton, 1979.

_____. *The Creepy Thing*. Houghton/Clarion, 1982.

_____. *Who's Seen the Scissors?* Dutton, 1975.

Knobler, Susan. *The Tadpole and the Frog*. Harvey, 1974.

Lisker, Sonia. *Lost*. Harcourt, 1975.

_____. *The Attic Witch*. Four Winds, 1973.

Mari, Iela and Enzo. *The Apple and the Moth*. Pantheon. 1970.

_____. *The Chicken and the Egg*. Pantheon, 1970.

Mari, Iela. *The Magic Balloon*. S. G. Phillips, 1969.

Mayer, Mercer. *A Boy, A Dog and A Frog*. Dial, 1967.

_____. *Frog, Where Are You?* Dial, 1969.

_____. *Frog on His Own*. Dial, 1973.

_____. *Frog Goes to Dinner*. Dial, 1974.

_____. *Bubble Bubble*. Parent's, 1973.

_____. *Two Moral Tales*. Dial, 1974.

_____. *Two More Moral Tales*. Dial, 1975.

_____. *Ac-Hoo!* Dial, 1976.

_____. *Oops!* Dial, 1977.

_____. *One Frog Too Many*. Dial, 1977.

Mayer, Mercer and Marianna Mayer. *A Boy, A Dog, A Frog and A Friend*. Dial, 1971.

_____. *Hiccup!* Dial, 1976.

_____. *Mine!* Simon and Schuster, 1970.

McPhail, David. *On, No, Go*. Atlantic, Little, 1973.

McTrusty, Ron. *Dandelion Year*. Harvey, 1974.

Mendoza, George. *The Inspector*. Doubleday, 1970.

Meyer, Rente. *Hide-and-Seek*. Bradbury, 1969.

Morris, Terry. *Goodnight, Dear Monster!* Knopf, 1980.

_____. *Lucky Puppy! Lucky Boy!* Knopf, 1980.

Ormerod, Jan. *Sunshine*. Lothrop, 1981.

_____. *Moonlight*. Lothrop, 1982.

Park, W. B. *Charlie-Bob's Fan*. Harcourt, 1981.

Remington, Barbara. *Boat*. Doubleday, 1975.

Ringi, Kjell. *The Magic Stick*. Harper & Row, 1969.

_____. *The Winner*. Harper & Row, 1969.

Roberts, Thom. *The Barn*. McGraw-Hill, 1975.

Ross, Pat. *Hi Fly*. Crown, 1974.

Sasaki, Isao. *Snow*. Viking, 1982.

Schick, Eleanor. *Making Friends*. Macmillan, 1969.

Shimin, Symion. *A Special Birthday*. McGraw-Hill, 1976.

Simmons, Ellie. *Cat*. David McKay, 1969.

_____. *Dog*. David McKay, 1967.

_____. *Family: A Book You Can Read Before You Know How*. David McKay, 1970.

Spier, Peter, *Noah's Ark*. Doubleday, 1977.

_____. *Peter Spier's Rain*. Doubleday, 1982.

Steiner, Charlotte. *I Am Andy*. Knopf, 1961.

Sugano, Yoshikatsu. *The Kitten's Adventure*. McGraw-Hill, 1971.

Sugia, Yutaka. *My Friend Little John and Me*. McGraw-Hill, 1973.

Snyder, Agnes. *The Old Man on Our Block*. Holt, 1964.

Tanaka, Hideyuki. *The Happy Dog*. Atheneum, 1983.

Turkle, Brinton. *Deep in the Forest*. Dutton, 1976.

Ueno, Noriko. *Elephant Buttons*. Harper & Row, 1973.

Ungerer, Tomi. *One, Two, Three*. Harper & Row, 1964.

_____. *One, Two, Where's My Shoe?* Harper & Row, 1964.

_____. *Snail, Where Are You?* Harper & Row, 1962.

Watson, Aldren. *The River*. Holt, 1973.

Wezel, Peter, *The Good Bird*. Harper & Row, 1964.

_____. *The Naughty Bird*. Harper & Row, 1967.

Wildsmith, Brian. *Brian Wildsmith's Circus*. Watts, 1970.

Winter, Paula. *The Bear and the Fly*. Crown, 1976.

_____. *Sir Andrew*. Crown, 1980.

Wondriska, William. *A Long Piece of String*. Holt, 1963.

Young, Ed. *Up a Tree*. Harper & Row, 1983.

CHAPTER TEN

The Art of Picture Books

Illustrators and Their Work

Developing an appreciation of illustrations in picture books is an aspect of sharing literature with children that should not be overlooked. According to Cianciolo(1976), "Wide and careful reading of books that are illustrated with beautiful paintings and designs will help the reader to acquire an appreciation for and an understanding of fine art" (p. 111). Cianciolo stresses the need for children to have opportunities to compare various artistic styles and the use of varying types of media, to be aware of the worth of different picture book artists, and to discriminate fine literature from that of lesser quality.

Even in the primary grades, children are capable of learning the terms, "author" and "illustrator" and learning what each contributes to the creation of the picture book, and how to locate the names of the author and illustrator on the book jacket/ cover and on the title page. (Teaching children to examine the title page is an important book handling skill. Many picture book artists begin the illustrations on the title page. Overlooking the title page may cause the reader to miss the introduction of a story.) Young children can become familiar with some authors and illustrators and can identify favorite creators as well as favorite works.

Before initiating a study of picture book authors/illustrators, the teacher needs to be aware of various sources of information. The following sources generally provide background information on authors and illustrators, listings of books authored/illustrated, and occasionally comments from the authors/illustrators themselves.

Block, Ann and Carolyn Riley(Eds.). *Children's Literature Review*. Gale Research Co. (Multiple Volumes)

Commire, Anne (Ed.). *Something About the Author*. Gale Research Co. (Multiple Volumes)

de Montreville, Doris and Elizabeth Crawford. *Junior Authors and Illustrators*. Wilson.

Hoffman, Miriam and Eva Samuels (Eds.). *Authors and Illustators of Children's Books; Writing on Their Lives and Works*. Bowker.

Hopkins, Lee Bennett. *Books Are By People*. Citation, 1969.

_____. *More Books By More People*. Citation, 1974.

Ward, Martha and Dorothy Marquardt. *Illustrators of Books for Young People*. Scarecrow, 1975.

Wintle, Justin and Emma Fisher. *The Pied Pipers*. Paddington Press, 1974 (interviews).

Language Arts, a journal published by the National Council of Teachers of English, has a monthly feature called "Profile" that discusses the work of a particular author or illustrator.

Each year, the August issue of *The Horn Book* magazine publishes biographical sketches and the acceptance speeches of the Caldecott and Newbery Award recipients.

The "Self-Portrait Collection" published by Addison-Wesley offers autobiographical picture books illustrated by the author. Those presently available in the series are: *Self Portrait: Margot Zemach* (1978), *Self Portrait: Erik Blevgad* (1979), *Self Portrait: Trina Schart Hyman* (1981), and *Self Portrait: Garth Williams*(1982). These first person narratives give added insight into the lives of the author/illustrator.

Publishers frequently have leaflets or bookmarks with biographical information, lists of books, and pictures of their authors and illustrators. These are available upon request from the publisher's publicity director.

Children (and teachers) are often very curious about authors and illustrators and their craft. To begin the study of a particular author/illustrator, a bulletin board with a picture of the person and some book jackets can serve as an introduction. (Many of the previously mentioned sources contain pictures.) A plentiful supply of books written and/or illustrated by the person is needed.

Children may want to write letters to the author/illustrator or send a cassette tape of questions. These can be sent in care of the publisher. Most will answer the children's letters in writing, and some will even return a tape.

Occasionally, a school might want to invite an author or illustrator to visit and speak to the children. Botham and Morris in the December, 1977 issue of *School Library Journal* offer these helpful suggestions for inviting an author/illustrator:

1. Have more than one person in mind in case your first choice in unavailable.
2. If you can't decide who to ask, publishers have lists of those who are willing to speak and will make suggestions.
3. Extend the invitation at least 2-3 months in advance.
4. Have your budget established in advance.
5. Extend the invitation through the publisher, addressed to the school and library services division.

It is better that the invitation be written rather than a telephone call. The letter should include the name of the desired speaker, the date of the meeting, the size and type of audience, the length of the talk, and the amount of money you can offer for travel and speaker's fees. Once you have received the author's acceptance, you can make specific arrangements regarding speaker's arrival time, accommodations, local transportation, and the like. Request publicity leaflets from the publisher. Generally, those who come to hear an author/illustrator speak wish to purchase a book and have it autographed. Order books well in advance from the publisher with the understanding that you will pay for those that are sold and return the remaining copies. It is especially important that everyone involved in the program be familiar with the author/illustrator and his/her works.

Many children might want to become involved in doing some illustrations of their own. This activity can be coordinated with the study of an illustrator or illustrators.

The collage technique is a style of art that can be studied in the primary grades. A collage is made by pasting a variety of materials that have been cut out or torn onto pages to form the illustration. Books by Ezra Jack Keats and Leo Lionni are excellent examples of this style, although their collages differ somewhat from each other in appearance. After children have experimented with various materials and made collages, they can write a story and illustrate it using the collage technique. Children might also enjoy viewing the film *Ezra Jack Keats*, available from Weston Woods. In this film, Keats explains how he uses materials to develop the collage style in his illustrations.

Children who are interested in drawing and learning how to get started might enjoy Ed Emberley's drawing books (see bibliography for a complete listing):

Ed Emberley's Drawing Book of Animals
Ed Emberley's Drawing Book of Faces
Ed Emberley's Drawing Book: Make a World
Ed Emberley's Great Thumbprint Drawing Book
Ed Emberley's Little Drawing Books: Farms, Weirdos, Birds, Trains

Emberley began with basic shapes and shows, through simplified step-by-step illustrations, how to add features and complete a drawing.

Upper primary grade children could view the Weston Woods sound filmstrip "How A Picture Book Is Made," narrated by illustrator Steven Kellogg. In this filmstrip, Kellogg gives some information about himself and explains the preparation of the illustrations for *The Island of Skog* from start to finished book. The technical information is clearly presented in a form children can understand. Reading of *The Island of Skog* should precede the viewing, and children would certainly want to reexamine it after seeing the filmstrip. Weston Woods also has available the sound filmstrip "The Island of Skog."

Children might also enjoy the sound filmstrip "Meet the Newbery Author: Arnold Lobel," distributed by Miller Brody/Random House. Lobel has received both Newbery and Caldecott Honor Book citations for his Frog and Toad stories. The filmstrip features a step-by-step explanation of his drawing techniques. Have available the four Frog and Toad books for reading before and after the filmstrip. Have the children compare these with other books by Lobel. Miller Brody/Random House also publishes the sound filmstrip of *Frog and Toad Together* and *Frog and Toad Are Friends*. The companion books to these are *Frog and Toad All Year* and *Days With Frog and Toad*.

Children frequently ask authors and illustrators where they get their ideas or why they draw the way they do. In his book *Cober's Choice*, Alan E. Cober has written a simple text explaining how he came to draw each picture to accompany his animal drawings. After reading the book and discussing the text and illustrations, children can do their own drawing and write a brief explanation to accompany it.

Children might also be involved in the creative process of illustration after viewing the film, *Ink, Paint, Scratch* by Robert Swarthe, produced by Little Red Filmhouse. This film shows how to create a film without using a camera and give a brief introduction to animation. A review in *Booklist* (December 1, 1979, p. 565) stated that even eight-year-olds were capable of viewing the film and using the technique. Children could make a short film as a group project, using a favorite story as the stimulus for the illustrations or stories they have written themselves.

Sample Illustrator Study

The suggestions given deal with the study of author/illustrator Jose Aruego. To introduce Aruego to the children, a bulletin board featuring one of his many animal characters would be appropriate.

217

There is a full-page picture of Aruego in *Language Arts* (May, 1977, p. 586). Have a large supply of his books available to read to the children and for them to read for themselves. (See listing below.) Give the children some brief biographical information: Jose Aruego was born in the Philippines; he was a lawyer before he became an illustrator. The sources cited earlier in this chapter will be helpful in supplying this information.

Ideas and Activities for Using the Books of Jose Aruego:

Look What I Can Do

1. Since this book is nearly wordless, children may wish to tell the story into the tape recorder. They can then listen to the versions of other children.
2. Play the game "Follow the Leader."
3. Have the children find out what a caribou looks like and learn other information about the animal.

We Hide, You Seek

1. This book also has very little text, which allows the children to tell their own story.
2. The illustrations will challenge the children to find the various animals camouflaged in their surroundings.
3. The book can lead to a science lesson on animals that rely on camouflage for protection.
4. The variety of animals that are depicted on the end papers of the book can lead to the study of some unusual animals.
5. A game of "Hide and Seek" can serve as a follow up to the sharing of the book.

A Crocodile's Tale

1. This is a Philippine folktale. Children can locate the Philippines on the map. The concept of "island" can be developed. Also, a discussion of the climate would be appropriate to this story.
2. The theme of the story is "gratitude." Discuss what this means and how the children can relate this to their own lives.

Leo the Late Bloomer

1. For a creative writing activity, have the children write a story about something that was hard for them to learn to do.
2. Have the children draw pictures of something that they would like to learn to do.

Milton the Early Riser

1. As a whole group, the children could make two charts: "Things to do when I get up early" and "Things I *shouldn't* do when I get up early."
2. The second chart could tie very well into a discussion of safety.
3. Find actual photos or informational books about pandas.

Owliver

1. Have the children write/dictate stories about what they want to be when they grow up. Tie this in to a lesson on various occupations.
2. Have the children dramatize the different emotions that Owliver acts out.

Three Friends

1. This book puts Milton, Leo and Herman together for a story and would be a good follow up to the books about the three characters individually.
2. The three friends have three exciting adventures which are told in pictures. Have children write stories about the three adventures.

Mushrooms in the Rain

This book is very appropriate for a sequencing activity. The children can put the animals in the order in which they appeared in the story, using picture cards or word cards.

Rum Pum Pum

1. This is an Indian folktale. Have the children find India on the map.
2. This story is very good for sequencing the events.

Marie Louise and Christophe, Marie Louise's Heydey, and *Runaway Marie Louise*

These stories are a little longer and more challenging to read. Have the children find out what a mongoose is and how it lives.

Gregory the Terrible Eater

1. Coordinate the book with a study of the four basic food groups.
2. Have the children write menus, both "junk" food and serious.

3. Prepare "junk" food meals, using papers, boxes, cans, and whatever the children can find.
4. Discuss our popular term "junk food" and make a chart of foods to avoid.
5. Also on the chart, the children could put pictures cut from magazines, candy wrappers, etc.
6. Make a class list of things each child doesn't like to eat. Then over a period of a week or two, have everyone including the teacher try *one* thing he/she doesn't like. Keep records of these experiences on the chart.

After children are familiar with some of Aruego's character they might write riddles about them for others to guess. For example:

My mother wants me to be an actor.
My father wants me to be a doctor
or a lawyer.
I want to be a firemen.
I am _____.

I am black and white.
I can sing and dance.
I like to get up early.
I am _____.

Children might also want to do paintings or drawings of their favorite Aruego characters. Teachers will want to add other ideas to the ones given here.

BIBLIOGRAPHY OF ARUEGO BOOKS

Written and Illustrated by Jose Aruego.

Juan and the Asuangs: A Tale of Philippine Ghosts and Spirits (Scribner, 1970).
The King and His Friends (Scribner, 1969).
Look What I Can Do (Scribner, 1971).
Pilyo the Piranha (Macmillan, 1971).
Symbiosis: A Book of Unusual Friendships (Scribner, 1970).

Written and Illustrated by Jose Aruego and Ariane Dewey (Aruego).

A Crocodile's Tale. (Scribner, 1972).
Two Group RAF: Adapted from a Hungarian Folk Tale (Macmillan, 1976).
We Hide, You Seek. (Greenwillow, 1979).

Written by Robert Kraus and Illustrated by Jose Aruego and Ariane Dewey (Aruego).

Leo the Late Bloomer. (Windmill, 1971).
Milton the Early Riser (Windmill, 1971).
Owliver (Windmill, 1972).
Herman the Helper (Windmill, 1974).
Three Friends (Windmill, 1975).
Boris Bad Enough (Windmill, 1976).
Noel the Coward (Windmill, 1977).
Musical Max (Windmill, 1979).
Another Mouse to Feed (Windmill, 1979).
Mert the Blurt (Windmill, 1980).

Adapted by Mirra Ginsburg and Illustrated by Jose Aruego and Ariane Dewey (Aruego).

The Chick and the Duckling (Macmillan, 1972).
How the Sun Was Brought to the Sky (Macmillan, 1974).
Mushroom in the Rain (Macmillan, 1974).
Two Greedy Bears (Macmillan, 1976).
The Strongest One of All (Greenwillow, 1977).
Where Does the Sun Go at Night? (Greenwillow, 1980).

Written by varied authors, illustrated by Jose Aruego.

Parakeets and Peach Pies (Kay Smith, Parent's, 1970).
Toucan Two, and Other Poems (Jack Prelutshy, Macmillan, 1970).
Whose Mouse Are You? (Robert Kraus, Macmillan, 1971).
What Is Pink? (Christina Rossetti, Macmillan, 1971).
The Day They Parachuted Cats on Borneo (Charlotte Pomerantz, Scott, 1971).
Good Night (Elizabeth Coatsworth, Macmillan, 1972).

Sea Frog, City Frog (Dorothy Van Woerkom, Macmillan, 1975).
Never Say Ugh to a Bug (Norma Farber, Greenwillow, 1979).

Written by varied authors, illustrated by Jose Aruego and Ariane Dewey (Aruego).

Marie Louise and Christophe (Natalie Savage Carlson, Scribner, 1974).
Marie Louise's Heyday (Natalie Savage Carlson, Scribner, 1975).
Runaway Marie Louise (Natalie Savage Carlson, Scribner, 1977).
If Dragon Flies Made Honey Poems (Edited by David Kherdian, Morrow, 1977).
Rum Pum Pum (Maggie Duff, Macmillan, 1978).
Mitchell Is Moving (Marjorie Weinman Sharmat, Macmillan, 1978).
Gregory the Terrible Eater (Mitchell Sharmat, Four Winds, 1980).
Lizard's Song (George Shannon, Greenwillow, 1981)
Dance Away (George Shannon, Greenwillow, 1982).

A format similar to the one suggested here can be applied to the study of other authors/illustrators.

REFERENCES

Botham, Jane and William C. Morris. "Authors and Artists as Speakers; Suggestions for   Hassle-Free Visits." *School Library Journal* (Dec. 1977): 27-29.
Cianciolo, Patricia J. *Illustrations in Children's Books.* (2nd ed.) Dubuque, Iowa: W.C.   Brown, 1976.
Cober, Alan E. *Cober's Choice.* New York: E.P. Dutton/Unicorn, 1979.
Emberley, Ed. *Ed Emberley's Drawing Book of Animals.* Little, Brown, 1970.
_____. *Ed Emberley's Drawing Book: Make a World.* Little, Brown, 1972.
_____. *Ed Emberley's Little Drawing Book: Birds.* Little, Brown, 1973.
_____. *Ed Emberley's Little Drawing Book: Farms.* Little, Brown, 1973.
_____. *Ed Emberley's Little Drawing Book: Trains.* Little, Brown, 1973.
_____. *Ed Emberley's Little Drawing Book: Weirdos.* Little, Brown, 1973.
_____. *Ed Emberley's Drawing Book of Faces.* Little, Brown, 1975.
_____. *Ed Emberley's Great Thumbprint Drawing Book.* Little, Brown, 1977.
_____. *Ed Emberley's Big Green Drawing Book.* Little, Brown, 1979.
_____. *Ed Emberley's Big Orange Drawing Book.* Little, Brown, 1980.
_____. *Dinosaurs! A Drawing Book.* Little, Brown, 1980.
Miller Brody/Random House. "Meet the Newbery Author: Arnold Lobel." For catalog and ordering information, write Random House School Division, 400 Hahn Road, Dept. 195A, Westminster, Maryland 21157.
Swarthe, Robert. *Ink, Paint, Scratch.* Little Red Filmhouse, 1979. (11 minutes).
Weston Woods.
  films: *Ezra Jack Keats*
        Robert McCloskey
        Maurice Sendak
  filmstrip: "How A Picture Book Is Made."
For catalog and ordering information, write Weston Woods, Weston, Connecticut 06883.